Preparing for Leadership

What It Takes
to Take the Lead

Preparing for Leadership

What It Takes to Take the Lead

Donna J. Dennis, Ph.D.
with
Deborah Dennis Meola

American Management Association

New York • Atlanta • Brussels • Chicago • Mexico City
San Francisco • Shanghai • Tokyo • Toronto • Washington, D.C.

Special discounts on bulk quantities of AMACOM books are available to corporations, professional associations, and other organizations. For details, contact Special Sales Department, AMACOM, a division of American Management Association, 1601 Broadway, New York, NY 10019.
Tel: 212-903-8316. Fax: 212-903-8083.
E-mail: specialsls@amanet.org
Website: www.amacombooks.org/go/specialsales
To view all AMACOM titles go to: www.amacombooks.org

This publication is designed to provide accurate and authoritative information in regard to the subject matter covered. It is sold with the understanding that the publisher is not engaged in rendering legal, accounting, or other professional service. If legal advice or other expert assistance is required, the services of a competent professional person should be sought.

Library of Congress Cataloging-in-Publication Data

Dennis, Donna J.
    Preparing for leadership : what it takes to take the lead / Donna J. Dennis with Deborah Dennis Meola.
        p. cm.
    Includes bibliographical references and index.
    ISBN 978-0-8144-1452-1
    1. Leadership. I. Meola, Deborah Dennis. II. Title.
    HD57.7.D473 2009
    658.4'092--dc22

                                                                                    2009007652

© 2009 American Management Association
All rights reserved.
Printed in the United States of America.

This publication may not be reproduced, stored in a retrieval system, or transmitted in whole or in part, in any form or by any means, electronic, mechanical, photocopying, recording, or otherwise, without the prior written permission of AMACOM, a division of American Management Association, 1601 Broadway, New York, NY 10019.

Printing number
10 9 8 7 6 5 4 3 2 1

CONTENTS

Acknowledgments

I have had the opportunity to know many wonderful leaders in my career; I draw on those relationships for this book. Bruce Avolio originally taught me to look at the relationships of leaders and their groups. He models the work he teaches and transforms the way I work with leaders. Sue Wheelan deserves thanks for her flexibility and encouragement as she deepened my understanding of groups. My professional colleagues, including Val Aguirre, Lauren Ashwell, Hope Greenfield, Mary Key, Katherine Kish, Pamela Rivera, Mary Ryan, Robb Most, Dick Quinn, and Randy Williams, as well as all the folks at the International Gestalt Center, but especially Sonia and Edwin Nevis, have influenced me. Curt Carlson encouraged me to finish my PhD many years ago and continues to support my work. Mary Lou Leib, Marianne Roy, Suzanne La Bombard, and Maureen Pryor showed me what it is like to be part of a stage four team. Jack Welch is well known as an excellent leader, but I want to acknowledge his contribution to my work, even in granting permission of his note in this book—he always is supportive and positive—which is a sign of a true leader!

Finally, to friends and family who listened while I "talked out" the ideas for this book—Anita Attridge, Karen Copeland, Rob Gilbert, and of course my entire family—thanks for your support.

Christina Parisi, the editor of this book, provided guidance and constant support. Thanks for supporting me through a fulfilling process.

Preparing for Leadership

What It Takes to Take the Lead

Introduction

Congratulations! You have been entrusted with the development of others—you are a leader. The satisfaction that comes from inspiring others to succeed is the reward awaiting a successful leader. Leaders do not spring into the world fully formed. In fact, it often takes successful leaders years to reach their stride. Leadership requires lifelong learning, flexibility to shift styles, and high levels of self-awareness and reflection. A sense of humor doesn't hurt either. The impact of strong leaders on an organization goes right to the bottom line; they can transform an organization to be resilient, growth oriented, and innovative. Poor leadership can be downright destructive, causing conflicts, turnover, and confusion in the workplace—even health issues in employees. In fact, bad leadership can cause more harm than no leadership at all, often destroying a piece of the company in the process. Leadership requires action to achieve results while balancing competing needs—a tough challenge, to be certain.

This book is a guide on leadership. It includes practical assessments, tips, and evaluations you can use. It will help you think about current challenges you face and possible solutions for dealing with those obstacles.

The Institute for Corporate Productivity (i4cp) conducts an annual survey of North American companies in which executives are asked to rank 120 different issues facing businesses. Leadership is consistently ranked the highest. In fact, leadership has landed in the number one spot every year since 1997.[1] Why is it the top business issue year after year? Why is it so difficult to lead other people? Why do companies spend millions annually to develop leaders? What about leadership is so elusive? What can you do as a leader to keep your impact high, and what new skills will you need to stay on top as a leader?

There are different ways to analyze leaders' performance to learn from their actions; it's possible to break out their behaviors and actually figure out what the actions of a good leader look like. Another option is to look at what is gained from good leadership: group satisfaction, productivity, goal attainment, and financial performance are a few of the things that come from strong leadership. Whichever measurement you prefer, the results are the same. Good leaders make a difference to the overall bottom line. Stated another way, it is worth your time to develop as a leader.

Whether you are a new leader or a seasoned professional, this book will help you face the issues of the current business climate. Here's a practical guide to align your leadership skills for today and tomorrow. The first step toward improving your own leadership skills is to assess your current situation. Ask yourself: What are the biggest obstacles to your role as a leader? Is it the fast pace of change in your workplace or increased globalization? Leaders often list challenges as obstacles to good leadership, such as balancing managerial control with a need to spark innovation, managing remote or virtual employees, and talent retention. These would be characterized as forces within the organization. When you look at the fast pace of change, mergers and acquisitions, and increased globalization, typically these are outside business forces that challenge leaders. Make a list of the current obstacles you face in your organization from inside or outside the company.

With these in mind, it is now possible to look at ways to increase your leadership effectiveness that will help you with these and any future trials you face.

What Is Leadership?

To lead people, walk beside them.

—Lao-tsu

You may not realize it, but you already have an image of what leadership looks like. If you brainstorm a list of exceptional political leaders over the course of history, you would probably name such figures as Alexander the Great, Julius Caesar, Napoleon Bonaparte, Abraham Lincoln, Winston Churchill, Franklin D. Roosevelt, Mahatma Gandhi, John F. Kennedy, Martin Luther King, Jr., Margaret Thatcher, Ronald Reagan—you probably can think of more.

What makes a good leader? What characteristics do good leaders all have in common? Where do they differ? Does the task make the leader or does the leader make the task? In short, what is leadership? The great leaders of history come from every walk of life; what unites them is their ability to inspire others to achieve beyond what is expected. When you look at leaders in the business world, the same characteristics hold true. There is not one career path to make a leader, but all good leaders share the desire to develop their business and their people—they know that both are essential to their effectiveness and their business results.

A Brief Review of History

The earliest views of leadership centered on a belief that leaders were born not made. This thinking fostered research designed to isolate the personality, as well as the physical and mental characteristics of leaders. It is interesting to think that one of Napoleon's greatest challenges to overcome was his height; an interesting early finding was that height was an important criterion for leadership! Early research concluded that key leadership traits are self-confidence, intelligence, determination, integrity, and sociability.[1] By 1983 Howard Gardner's concept of multiple intelligences[2] had surfaced, followed by Daniel Goleman's work on emotional intelligence, which stressed the importance of awareness of self and others and relationship skills as key components of leadership.[3] During this time period, personality research also described leadership traits, such as arrogance, that are detrimental to leadership effectiveness. [4]

Ultimately, leadership research expanded beyond an examination of the individual leader to include the group or culture the leader influences. One aspect of this research focused on relationships between the leader and followers. James MacGregor Burns[5] and those who succeeded him believed that leadership was a process that focused on the performance of followers and also the development of followers to their fullest potential.[6] Studies of group dynamics as well as concepts about shared leadership helped organizations get the best results. Craig Pearce and Jay Conger showed that shared leadership has a greater influence on team effectiveness than the more traditional leadership approaches.[7] All of this work focuses on the group's productivity and development rather than a single focus on the leader.

The good news is that whatever your personality profile or individual characteristics, you can be an effective leader—and, thank goodness, there's no longer a height requirement. The differentiating factors can be assessed, trained, and developed that contribute to making great leaders even better. What can be taken from this quick review of leadership history is that leadership has become very complex. There are many variables that will impact your success. Just to list a few:

- Your personality
- The organization's culture
- Your followers or the group you work with (skills, personalities, understanding of roles)

American Management Association
www.amanet.org

- The distance between members of the group geographically and culturally
- The goals you must achieve
- The resources you have to accomplish the goals
- Your leadership skills
- Technical skills
- Technological support for accomplishment of goals
- Special considerations in your organization, e.g., multicultural workforce

How you pull all these qualities together will determine your success.

Transformational Leadership

Bruce Avolio and Francis Yammarino are among those who have shown that certain types of leadership behaviors produce better results in every setting and business sector. That is, whether you work in a factory or an educational setting, there are leaders who respond to their followers' needs, which in turn produces better results. These leaders are known as *transformational*.[8] Transformational leaders look at each member of their staff and help them grow and develop into leaders in their own right. Transformational leaders respond to individual followers' differences and needs, and then empower each individual to align his or her objectives and goals to the larger organization.

A model of leadership influenced by the theory of Transformational Leadership includes five main components necessary for a strong leader: Communicating Direction, Inspirational Motivation, Problem Resolution, Building the Team, and Trust (see Figure 1.1). The core of this model is trust because this is the foundation of any effective leader.

Trust

The success of Ricky Gervais's BBC show *The Office*, as well as the U.S. spin-off, attests to the popularity of depicting the boss as an insufferable moron. The

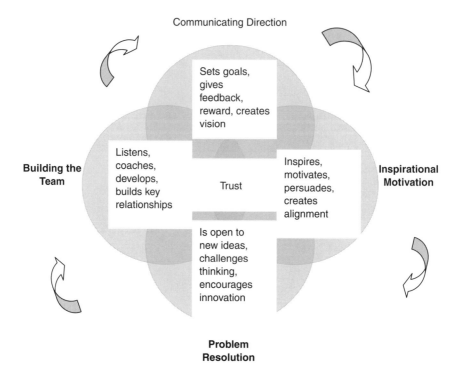

Communicating Direction

Sets goals, gives feedback, reward, creates vision

Building the Team

Listens, coaches, develops, builds key relationships

Trust

Inspires, motivates, persuades, creates alignment

Inspirational Motivation

Is open to new ideas, challenges thinking, encourages innovation

Problem Resolution

Figure 1.1 Model of leadership influenced by transformational leadership theory.

lead character, played by Steve Carrell in the United States, does not hesitate to lie to his employees to try to further his own cause. It makes for funny television because it is based on the reality that only about one-third of office workers consider their own leaders to be honest. Life often is more extreme than art; just think of headlines involving such well-known business people as Kenneth Lay of Enron or Dennis Kozlowski of Tyco. These two businessmen turned criminal in their deceit and show just how far the trust deficit can go in the business world today. This is unfortunate, because trustworthiness is the top attribute that people want in their leaders.

James Kouzes and Barry Posner have surveyed over 75,000 people around the world on the topic of credibility and found that people consistently say they want leaders who are "honest, forward-looking, competent and inspiring."[9] When you think about your own idea of what makes a good leader, you'll probably find that qualities such as integrity, honesty, and trust are most important to you as well. This is because a team that operates with trust as its foundation is able to provide a sense of reliability and confidence that other teams lack. Therefore, it is important to recognize what helps to encourage trust and what destroys it.

══ SCENE ══

Suppose your company is about to lay off 10 percent of the workforce. As a manager, you want to try to maintain trust throughout this process. Isabel approaches you in the break room and says, "I heard that there might be a layoff. Do you know anything about this?"

You do know something about the layoff, but do you fill her in? What are some possible answers to this question? Which response will help maintain your trust? Here are some ideas:

- "Yes, there are discussions of layoffs, but nothing is firm right now."
- "You know management has been looking for ways to run our business more efficiently for some time—I think this is just more of that initiative."
- "No, I have not heard anything."
- "I am not at liberty to discuss that right now."

Answers might vary depending on the internal situation. Sometimes managers are advised of a layoff and specifically told not to tell their direct reports. While internal Human Resource people will coach managers on what they are and are not allowed to do and say, many leaders who want to keep their trust and credibility high will find a way to tell their employees something without betraying Human Resources. The worst choice in this list of answers is to totally deny the rumor— this is a flat-out lie, and the employee will feel betrayed because of it. When the culture in the organization is one of distrust, like during times of downsizing or restructuring, it is critical that managers tell their employees as much as they can as soon as they can.

If employees believe their leader cannot be trusted they will divert energy toward "covering their backs," which can detract from employees' work performance. Good leaders recognize that trust results in higher performance and good citizenship. This is supported by the findings of a large meta-analysis that summarized research over the past four decades.[10] In this study, the author, Kurt Dirks, finds that trust can positively impact an organization with benefits like increased cooperation, more collaboration, more pride in the work, increased innovation, and reciprocity in negotiations, as well as affect the positive attitudes of employees, which in turn helps customer relations. Conversely, when trust is not present or is lost through a betrayal, the business impacts include distress and anger in the workforce, which leads to decreased productivity. People spend time trying to seek justice or put things "right" rather than on the business mission.

Trust can be hard to foster as part of a regular work group, and it comes as no surprise that when groups work virtually, trust becomes a bigger issue because it is harder to gain and easier to erode when working in multiple locations. Regardless of circumstances, though, people want a leader that they can admire, a leader they can emulate, a leader they can trust. Chapter 3 will focus on ways to develop trust and respect among teams. While trust is essential, the four other components that build from a leader focused on trust are critical too.

Transformational Leadership Model Components

Communicating Direction

The best leaders not only set goals and milestones for themselves and their teams they also communicate these goals to all the stakeholders. The leader needs to have a vision and to be able to articulate that to the other members. Further, when specific details are added to the vision, it helps employees reach their goals, and this direction is critical to successful leadership. The leader also assesses the employees' understanding of the work and figures out what they need to develop further understanding or skill. The leader provides personal attention to each person in the group so that everyone is aligned with work goals and direction.

Analyze your own language to make your communications effective. An optimistic explanatory style should be used for both adverse and positive events. The number one reason people give up is they believe in the permanence of the bad event. People who resist helplessness believe bad events are merely temporary setbacks or challenges to overcome. For good events, just the opposite approach should be taken by leaders. Don't water down an effort by describing your team as "lucky" or having a "good day." Rather, speak in universal terms: "I knew this team could do this; you guys are always tops." As a leader, try to find permanent and universal causes for good events and temporary, specific causes for misfortune.

Through continuous communication, leaders monitor goals, provide feedback that is both positive and constructive, and empower employees while accomplishing organizational goals.

══ S C E N E ══

Spencer is a manager from a research firm. He told his staff, "We are all washed up. We will never get this thing through the FDA approval process." This statement uses general, universal language that leaves little hope. Instead, try: "We're all exhausted. Let's try to figure out later why the FDA did not approve this thing and get them the information they need."

Conversely, when the team did get one of their products approved, Spencer said, "Wow, we were lucky today! I can't believe we snuck that one through."

Instead try: "This team is the most hardworking team I have ever met. I knew you would do what it takes to get this thing through to the end!"

Inspirational Motivation

In the Scene, the manager, Spencer, not only communicated directions, he tried to motivate and inspire with his language. Inspirational motivation is the ability to influence others. For individuals to° give leaders their best work, they need to feel that the leader truly wants the best for them as individuals. This is achieved by leaders who successfully communicate and, thus, inspire their associates. These leaders reward and recognize people for their accomplishments. In addition, they also address the associate's sense of self-worth to engage him or her in true commitment and involvement in the effort at hand.

When leaders inspire, they are able to motivate employees to do more than those employees originally intended and often even more than they thought possible. Leaders empower followers and pay attention to their individual needs and personal development, helping associates to develop their own leadership potential. Through motivation, leaders are able to encourage innovation in their teams. This is important if setbacks or problems occur along the way.

Problem Resolution

One thing is certain: Problems will develop. Strong leaders can avoid or resolve problems because they have the ability to challenge their own thinking as well as that of the team, to develop new ideas, interesting solutions, and innovative approaches. Leaders know how to ask thought-provoking questions and listen to the answers; they challenge the status quo and stimulate creativity to better handle problems that arise.

Good leaders are instrumental in removing obstacles to achieve goals and seek input from those who are closest to the work. This can take the form of talking with senior people in the organization to "clear the way" for involvement with another department. It could mean making sure resources are available to the team or that budget is released for the project. Leaders remove barriers to productive work and cooperate to solve problems. This enables the team to move forward. Notice that all the components in this model encompass the development of the individuals on the team as well as the group as a whole; in this way the team grows as each individual grows.

Building the Team

Since so much of the work in today's business world is done in groups, an effective leader knows just how to build a team. This includes the ability to develop each individual on the team to work better as an entire group. This is done through joining the right people for a task, then assisting them and empowering them to pursue a goal. If you have the luxury of picking your team, make sure that you include individuals with the skills you need for the job but also with the ability to work together with different people. A leader will also help the team develop key relationships and manage any conflicts. Leaders build relationships with all key stakeholders. They think about their actions

---

═══ SCENE ═══

A virtual team at an international bank included the leader from France, a systems expert from London, two accounting specialists—one from Hong Kong and one from the United States—and a designer from Singapore. When the team "met" on their conference call, the same dynamic always took place. The leader, Françoise, asked a question of the group, and the U.S. specialist, Kate, started talking. Kate answered the question, and then threw in all the questions she had collected in the last few weeks. She left little room for the other team members to speak. Fortunately, Kate only stayed on the international line for one-half hour, as it was early in the morning in her time zone and Kate had to transition to get her kids off to school. When she hung up, the leader realized the conversation changed. Instantly, the others on the team would begin to speak. The specialist in Hong Kong would often have a different perspective than Kate, and that led the designer to chime in with design issues and the U.K. systems expert with system issues to the solution the U.S. team member had suggested. What should the team leader do?

In this case, the leader tried a new approach, and on the next phone call Françoise posed specific questions to each member of the team before opening up the discussion to comments from all. On this team, there were cultural concerns as well as distance concerns that made the leader build the team in a very structured, deliberate way to ensure success.

---

in terms of the impact on people and groups or systems and then choose actions that will produce the best results for the organization.

As a leader, the context will change your responses.

Context of Leadership

The ingredients of a good leader do not change, but you will see your focus shift as the context of your leadership changes. Review the unique challenges that you face in your business. You might see that if the context of these obstacles were to change, your leadership responses would change, too.

Consider the highly successful technical expert in a marketing or sales group: Tricia is seen as high performing, so she's offered a promotion because of her obvious success in her current position. However, if Tricia continues doing what made her successful in the current job, it will not guarantee her success in the next job. In fact, it's likely to guarantee frustration and maybe even failure. Why? Because the new job requires a different set of skills, competencies, tools, and approaches. The context of the challenges has changed.

In this example, the change involves the task of the job, but in the earlier case, the contextual challenge was a virtual team. Over the distance, emails and text messages can change the cues a leader receives. Trust is even more difficult to gain on virtual assignments, and it is much easier to lose. It is important to check that all parties have the same understanding and that messages are not lost in translation. Leaders who discuss with their team what is required and specify the conditions and rewards others will receive ensure good communication. This will help their employees develop their full potential.

A change in the way companies now hire and promote managers can also cause contextual challenges. In a more traditional work world, leaders were always the most senior people. Today, often young people are tasked with leading those with more seniority. This can cause serious challenges for the team and the leader. If there are generational issues involved, thoughtful leadership is essential. Here's a brief summary of the attributes for each leadership characteristic (Figure 1.2).

Leaders:

1. Serve as a Role Model	Admired, respected, and trusted.
2. Communicate Direction	Envision and then communicate the goal or results to be achieved.
3. Build the Team	Enlist, enable, and empower the right people and resources to pursue goals. Understand the importance of developing the group as a high-performing team. Build key relationships and manage conflict.
4. Inspire Others, Motivate, Influence	Energize people to pursue goals. Know what motivates each person, how to influence and persuade others.
5. Solve Problems and Get Results	Evaluate progress and provide reinforcing or redirecting feedback.
	Ensure technical obstacles are overcome and people problems are resolved so that the goals are achieved. Encourage innovation and creativity by challenging thinking, supporting appropriate risk taking.

Figure 1.2 Leadership characteristics/attributes summary.

LEADERSHIP SELF-ASSESSMENT

Here's a chance for you to evaluate your leadership strengths and development needs. If you are not currently leading a group, you can answer based on past experiences—it need not be a "fresh" leadership role. You can even go back to some experience in high school or college. If any examples still don't come to mind, you can answer how you think you would behave in each of these situations. There is no "right" or "wrong" answer. Rather, there will be things that are easy for you and areas where you can improve.

Assess items 1 through 20 below and rate each item in terms of how frequently you use the behavior.

1	2	3	4	5
Never	Rarely	Sometimes	Often	Always

_____ 1. I show others that I am self-confident.

_____ 2. I think about the moral and ethical implications of my decisions.

_____ 3. I have created a sense of purpose or mission in my group.

_____ 4. I communicate clear direction or vision for the group.

_____ 5. I am enthusiastic and positive about what needs to be accomplished.

_____ 6. I find ways to overcome obstacles.

_____ 7. I plan carefully.

_____ 8. I actively address problems and make clear decisions.

_____ 9. I encourage open communication and trust with everyone.

_____ 10. I look for ways to help others increase productivity and loyalty.

_____ 11. I demonstrate personal energy, initiative, and integrity.

_____ 12. I provide the group with information, time, and resources to do their jobs.

_____ 13. I actively address conflicts with others.

_____ 14. I make fair decisions in my group.

_____ 15. I respond quickly and provide guidance to associates.

_____ 16. I build relationships with key stakeholders.

_____ 17. I ask others about what they think when I am trying to solve problems.

_____ 18. I find ways of developing others.

_____ 19. I make sure others are respected.

_____ 20. I build on the strengths of my associates.

Total: Never_____ Rarely_____ Sometimes_____ Frequently _____ Always_____

American Management Association
www.amanet.org

Another way to assess where you are on your leadership journey is to see if there is a pattern to your responses. For each section consider the highest score you could have achieved then look at your actual score. This will help you identify your strengths and development needs.

Communicate Direction   Possible 20   Actual_____

3. Sense of purpose

4. Communicate direction

5. Enthusiastic and positive about what needs to be accomplished

7. Plan carefully

Build the Team   Possible 20   Actual_____

9. Open communication and trust

13. Address conflicts

16. Build relationships with key stakeholders

19. Others are respected

Inspire Others   Possible 15   Actual_____

10. Increase productivity and loyalty

18. Developing others

20. Build on strengths of others

Solve Problems / Get Results   Possible 20   Actual_____

6. Find ways to overcome obstacles

7. Plan carefully

12. Provide the group with information, time, and resources to get their work done

15. Respond quickly, provide guidance

17. Ask others what they think when solving problems

*Leadership Character   Possible 20   Actual*_____

1. Self-confident

2. Think about the moral and ethical implications of decisions

11. Demonstrate personal energy, initiative, and integrity

14. Decisions are fair

*Total Possible   100   Actual*_____

Strengths: (my highest scores)

_____

_____

_____

Development Needs: (my lowest scores)

_____

_____

_____

■ Career Enhancement Tool ■
Mentors

Part of your challenge as a leader is to increase your ability to assess your impact on others, to "read" how your behavior has influenced others. This can be accomplished through self-assessments like the one you just completed. Another opportunity to grow your leadership skills is to find a mentor to guide and coach you.

Senior leaders often say no one gives them honest feedback. This can be cultivated with the ability to encourage others to point out what you are doing well and what needs to improve. This is where a mentor can help.

A mentor is a trusted person who can advise you on personal or professional matters. A mentor serves as teacher, sponsor, guide, exemplar, and counselor.

A mentor can help with basic advice like goal setting, performance feedback, and brainstorming solutions to problems. The benefits of a good mentor, however, go way beyond these tasks. Often a mentor can warn of a problem or protect you politically within an organization. This person should see your strengths and inspire you to continue in the hardest of times. But he or she should also verbalize your weaknesses and help you develop as a leader. Finally, if necessary, a mentor can provide a critical introduction or referral if you should need outside help or to transition to another position of leadership.

It may sound like a good mentor is impossible to find, but if you consider a few things prior to selecting a mentor, you too can have a successful relationship. Consider if the person listens well and asks probing questions. Like a coach, a good mentor doesn't tell you the answers but guides you through the provoking questions to reach your own answers. A good mentor is not the person who says, "That reminds me of a story" and shifts the focus to him- or herself, rather a person who uses his or her experiences and your own to relate to your dilemmas and challenges. Above all, a mentor provides encouragement; he or she is a fan of yours. A mentor can help you calibrate where you need to focus your developmental efforts and give you honest feedback as you work on your leadership goals.

Take a minute before you move on to Chapter 2 to review the components of a strong leader. Come up with a plan to find a mentor for your own leadership development.

_____

_____

_____

Leadership Style:
Fit Your Style to Your Group

If your actions inspire more, do more and become more, you are a leader.

—John Quincy Adams

As leaders, you juggle many roles: You are the leader of a group, but you are also a member of your manager's team; you are a peer to others, sometimes across different geographies, departments, or functions. You may have a role to play with vendors or partners in other companies. Customers have expectations of you and create another role for you to balance. Of course, there are the many roles you play outside of work. When style is the topic, leaders wear many different hats. Consider your home life and the various styles you use with your children. (Even if you don't have children, think back to when you were the child.) As a parent, the way you treat a 4-year-old in your family and the way you treat a teen are decidedly different. Parents of twins comment that they need to treat each child differently. The point is that you are already using variety of styles for different people, depending on what each one needs in order to get the results you want. In this chapter, a structure will surround those choices you make when working with your various groups.

A basic premise is that you and your group have tasks that you must get done. It turns out that groups mature or develop through predictable stages and that effective leaders shift their styles depending on the developmental stage the group is in, just like parents shift their styles with children of differing stages of development. Sue Wheelan, the author of many books and research studies on group development, provides an excellent way to view groups.[1] The role of the leader in guiding groups through stages of development is not often taught to leaders. You will increase your effectiveness if you recognize the stage of your group and then match your style to their stage.

How Leaders Lead in Each Stage of Group Development

Stage One Leaders

Stage one of the development process is that the group or individual doesn't know much about how to be competent. If someone in your group wants to make a clay pot, you will need someone to demonstrate and actually teach that individual how to work with the wheel and the clay. In stage one of group development, members need leaders who are clear about goals and deliverables and who assign roles and responsibilities to each person in the group. Leaders are more directive than participative, and decision making is controlled by the leader. Visually, a picture might look like Figure 2.1.

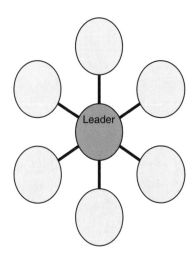

Figure 2.1 Stage one leader.

The leader is central. He or she directs the action and decision making because the individuals in the group are not capable of doing either one themselves. In a business setting, it might be described as the "training" stage for a new group. Group members need the leader to direct them because they do not yet know the ins and outs of the work or the corporate culture. Their experience is not at a stage where they can participate at the same level as the leader in making decisions or assigning tasks. The leader should encourage questions at this stage of development because that will help the individual or group progress to the next level more quickly. The leader monitors and gives feedback with the goal of moving the group to stage two of development.

Stage Two Leaders

This stage is often similar to adolescence in human development where group members want more independence than they had in stage one, but they may not be quite ready. Roles and decision making, power, status, and communications structures are clarified in this stage. Efforts to redistribute power begin to occur as well. These are all necessary for development to occur. This can feel like conflict (just like parenting a teenager); however, it is actually a positive sign of growth and independence. Leaders can experience this stage as a real challenge; often, they perceive conflict as resistance to their authority and therefore interpret it as negative. The leader may respond by creating rules, policies, and procedures to help enforce his or her way of doing things. Some leaders withdraw from the conflict. Much of the conflict, however, is about things that go beyond the role of the leader. In essence, the conflict with and about the leader is a way for the group to discuss who can have input into decisions. Figure 2.2 shows this graphically.

The leader's role in this stage is critical. If the leader avoids the direct reports or engages in debate without resolutions that work for everyone, the group will remain in stage two. If an individual is critical of the leader's decision, and the leader does not address these comments in a constructive way, the leader misses the chance to move the group on to stage three.

No leader wants everyone coming to her for every decision or action. Moving individuals to a developmental level where other options are possible is the goal. So what is the right response to a group in stage two? Group

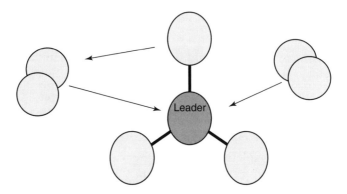

Figure 2.2 Stage two leader.

members have some skills, but they aren't ready for total independence. They may lack the confidence to take on total responsibility for the work they need to do. Here are some choices to consider:

1. Continue to provide direction.
2. Try their ideas.
3. Encourage them to keep trying; offer a lot of support.
4. Help them see what needs to be done to get the best results.

You are likely to do all of the above. Think of your role as consultative. You do want teams to move through this stage. However, it's not uncommon to experience conflict about readiness. Sometimes leaders personalize stage two differences in opinions. The result is defensiveness or attacks from members of the group that only escalate conflict. Just remember: Conflict can be a good thing. Bruce Avolio, a leading researcher in the field of leadership, comments that conflict is the "highest form of human communication."[2] Working through conflict increases group cohesion and trust, which makes it possible for the group to focus on strategies to achieve shared goals. For inexperienced leaders this can be a daunting task. Even experienced leaders find that delays in conflict resolution result in more problems and keep the team permanently in stage two.

Organizations that get stuck in stage two are terrible places to work, with lots of unresolved conflicts and "gotcha" behaviors. Individuals stuck in stage two find ways to avoid helping one another even at the cost of customer service or profitability goals.

Stage Three Leaders

In stage three, leaders are participative with teams in accomplishing tasks. Since managers cannot perform every task, delegation and power sharing is necessary and indicative of an effective leadership style. Goals and roles are clear, so the leader's role is less prominent. While the leader is still necessary for coordination, that coordination function is now shared among members and the leader. By this time, members facilitate meetings or portions of meetings. They give reports about subgroup meetings and about tasks that have been accomplished between meetings. Whether working individually or as a group, the members are involved in the decision making and conflict resolution as well as looking for new business opportunities, negotiation, buffering conflicts, and image management within the larger organization. See Figure 2.3.

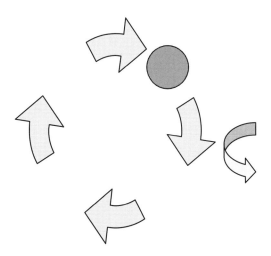

Figure 2.3 Stage three leader.

═══ **S C E N E** ═══

Consider that Tania is the manager of a technology group. Her staff is experienced and has been working together over two years. The group is divided into teams that support different applications, and they are aligned to different corporate functions such as Sales, HR, R&D, and Marketing. Tania has taken a well-deserved vacation, six hours away from her home office. While enjoying her vacation, she receives a call from her manager. Another huge corporate initiative is to be launched, and it will impact staffing and resources in their group. Tania's manager needs a plan and proposed budget two days after she returns from her vacation. What does she do?

In a stage three team, the leader engages the group in problem resolution. She involves the team in what needs to be done, then they get it done. Tania decides to set up a conference call and get the ball rolling, so she is certain the project will be ready when she returns. The group sets the goals clearly, divides up the work into sub-teams, and decides they will post it on a group site so that everyone can see what has been accomplished. Tania is able to enjoy the rest of her vacation with occasional glances at the computer to check in.

In short, members assume many of the functions performed solely by the leader in stages one and two. The leader operates in more egalitarian ways as all members of the team share responsibility. Leaders who support, compliment, and praise members' efforts to share in leadership will increase the likelihood of group and individual success.

Stage Four Leaders

Leaders now think about delegation as a development tool, not just as a way to get work off their desk. Leaders continue to act as consultants, as needed. In general, however, they participate along with members to achieve objectives and team success. They continue to monitor team processes, especially for signs of regression, and they continue to build relationships with stakeholders outside of their immediate group and get resources the team needs to do its work. According to Sue Wheelan, leading group development expert, stage four leaders "get to relax a bit."[3] Things should run smoothly; when conflict occurs, the group resolves it quickly. Team members have taken on responsibilities and are actively pursuing group goal achievement. Leaders find a key challenge in this stage is to keep employees motivated and engaged. Figure 2.4 represents this graphically.

═══ SCENE ═══

Stanley is the Division President for a small medical-devices division within a larger corporation. His staff consists of eight people who are the heads of the various functions, including finance, HR, operations, and sales. He has been in this position for over five years and has replaced several of the staff, some because they were promoted and some because they left the company. The current group has been together for three years.

Meetings run smoothly for the most part, and the division's business results hit their targets. Recently, the company raised the bar on financial targets needed this year. It looks aggressive, and Stanley does not even know if it's possible to reach the goal. As preparation for the meeting to discuss how to meet the new target, he asks each vice president to prepare to give his or her ideas on how best to accomplish the goal. Each of the VPs has set up meetings to gather data and complete a comprehensive planning process. Stanley decides to spend his time talking to a few key customers and some peers in other divisions.

During the day-long off-site meeting, Stanley joins his group, asking questions and discussing options. As the meeting draws to a close, there is need for follow-up, which Stanley is able to delegate. Then he sets a date for the next meeting. He plans to monitor the work, but this team is quite capable of working together to reach the target.

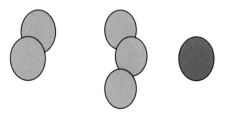

Figure 2.4 Stage four leader.

To summarize, you will use different approaches with different groups depending on the stage of development the group is in. In the beginning (stage one group), provide lots of structure, knowing that as the team grows it will come to a point in its journey when it will push back and want more autonomy. Begin to empower at that stage, building to a place where they are not so heavily relying on you as a leader. Over time, increase your consultative role.

Keep your checklist of leadership behaviors from Chapter 1 clearly in mind and demonstrate those behaviors. Another way to view this is that your approach will move from mostly telling to increasing amounts of asking, listening, or empowering (see Figure 2.5). Remember that your approach needs to change based on the level and assignment of the team.

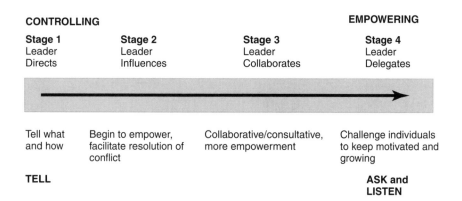

Figure 2.5 Leadership continuum.

CASE A: The Superstar Sales Performer

Rupal is an excellent territory manager; she just won the President's Award because she exceeded all of her sales targets. When the VP of Sales congratulates her, the VP suggests that she would make a great sales manager. She would lose some revenue initially, but her longer term goal is a position of leadership in the company, so she needs to leave direct sales and get on the management career path. This is a great opportunity for Rupal. She is about to meet with her sales team for the first time. Some of them have been selling for a long time and have never been as successful as she has, although all of them have met their targets.

It looks fairly straightforward to Rupal. She will just teach them how she does it, and they will improve their results. It's a simple matter of showing them how to replicate her success!

- What stage is Rupal's team in?
- Is she approaching her leadership role effectively?

CASE B: The HR Director

Jason is the new HR director. He transferred from another division and is known for being very direct in his interactions with others. His feedback is timely and specific. He has been successful with a variety of projects. This promotion, however, is a challenge because the team is accustomed to working very collaboratively, and that is not Jason's preferred style. Jason thinks collaboration is too time-consuming. He likes to assign work and have a project plan with milestones set and then just execute the plan. He thinks this increases accountability for everyone.

The team feels that its success is due to the interactions they have with one another, and their results are good because of their collaboration. They draw on one another's experience and learn from what each brings. They are concerned about what they have heard about Jason. They are meeting with Jason this afternoon. The team feels that if he tries to tell them what to do, they will need to "push back." Jason has heard the team might be argumentative.

- What stage of development is Jason's team in?
- Is he approaching the team effectively?

Leaders as Members of a Group or Team

Effective group members support the leader's efforts to coordinate and facilitate the group. Effective team members volunteer to perform tasks that need to be done. They are actively engaged with the leader to do the best work for the team and the organization. Remember that leadership requires relationships with the others in the group. As members of a group, you have the ability to make the leader highly successful; as a leader you can put the group in the position of doing its best work through your support, feedback, and encouragement. As a team member, use all of the same behaviors you utilized as the team leader to create a high-performing team.

Managing Up

Part of your challenge as a leader is not only to lead your group but also to "manage up." The people above you have expectations of you as well as the people you lead. You may have experienced being pulled in both directions—those above you have different goals than those below. The following scene will offer some insights.

═══ S C E N E ═══

Juan is new on the job. He thought he would like his boss when he joined the company, but now he isn't too happy with his boss's style. He feels micromanaged. In meetings, Juan tries to impress the boss with his understanding of the issues, but the boss cuts him off. Juan thinks his boss does not facilitate the meetings well. Juan likes the two people under him, but his boss feels he should be tougher with these two and give them more direct feedback. Juan thinks this will just upset the dynamic.

What can Juan do in this situation? What rules is he violating? What could he do to have a better relationship with his boss?

There are many ways to communicate that you support your boss. Some suggestions include the following:

- Work diligently to support the organizational goals.
- Take responsibility for your projects—the successes and the failures.
- Tackle problems head on.
- Handle crises rapidly.
- Overcome resistance to change.

Look at the following checklist to see where you fall as an effective member of the teams at your organization.

EFFECTIVE MEMBER CHECKLIST

Please read the statements below. Circle the number that most accurately describes your response to the statement. Use the following key to respond to each statement.

1	2	3	4
disagree strongly	disagree to some extent	agree to some extent	agree strongly

Section I

1. I avoid blaming others for group problems.

   1   2   3   4

2. I assume that every group member is trying to do a good job.

   1   2   3   4

3. I treat people as individuals and don't make assumptions about them based on my preconceived notions about people like them.

   1   2   3   4

4. I do not get bogged down in interpersonal issues or personality conflicts.

   1   2   3   4

Section I Score_____

Section II

5. I encourage the process of goal, role, and task clarification.

   1   2   3   4

6. I encourage the use of effective problem-solving and decision-making procedures.

   1   2   3   4

7. I encourage the group to outline, in advance, the strategies that will be used to solve problems and make decisions.

   1   2   3   4

8. I work to ensure that decisions and solutions are implemented and evaluated.

   1   2   3   4

9. I encourage norms that support productivity, innovation, and freedom of expression.

   1   2   3   4

10. I encourage the use of effective conflict management strategies.

   1   2   3   4

11. I support division of labor necessary to accomplish goals.

                                        Section II Score:_____

Section III

12. I work to ensure that the input and feedback of every member is heard.

   1   2   3   4

13. I work to ensure that we all have a chance to demonstrate our competence and skills in the group.

   1   2   3   4

14. I discourage any group tendency to adopt excessive or unnecessary norms.

   1   2   3   4

15. I am, and encourage others to be, cooperative.

   1   2   3   4

16. In conflict situations, I communicate my views clearly and explicitly.

   1   2   3   4

17. I respond cooperatively to others who are behaving competitively.

   1   2   3   4

                                        Section III Score_____

Section IV

18. I act, and encourage others to act, in the best interests of the group.

   1   2   3   4

19. When members contribute good ideas, I express my appreciation.

   1   2   3   4

20. I encourage and work to achieve mutually agreeable solutions to conflict.

    1   2   3   4

21. I support the leader's efforts to coordinate and facilitate group goal achievement.

    1   2   3   4

22. I offer advice to the leader when I think the advice will be helpful.

    1   2   3   4

Section IV Score_____

Section V

23. I have negotiated, or would be willing to negotiate, with other groups and individuals to help my group obtain needed resources.

    1   2   3   4

24. I share information and impressions I have about other parts of the organization with the group.

    1   2   3   4

25. I encourage the group not to overwhelm itself with too much external information or demands.

    1   2   3   4

26. I talk positively about my group with outsiders.

    1   2   3   4

27. I keep other members of the organization informed about what my group is doing.

    1   2   3   4

Section V Score_____

Section VI

28. When members stray off the task, I diplomatically try to bring the discussion back to the task.

    1   2   3   4

29. I go along with norms that promote group effectiveness and productivity.

   1   2   3   4

30. I encourage high performance standards.

   1   2   3   4

31. I expect the group to be successful and productive.

   1   2   3   4

32. I encourage innovative ideas.

   1   2   3   4

33. I use what I have learned about group development and productivity to help my group become effective.

   1   2   3   4

34. I encourage the group to frequently assess and alter its functioning, if necessary.

   1   2   3   4

35. I volunteer to perform tasks that need to be done.

   1   2   3   4

Section VI Score_____

Total Minimum Score: 35
Total Maximum Score: 140

My Score:_____

What's Your Overall Membership Quotient?

Total Score	Your Membership Grade
126+	A
112–125	B
98–111	C

What Are Your Section Scores?

Section I: Attitudes and Feelings

Total Score	Your Grade
14+	A
12–13	B
10–11	C

Section II: Processes and Procedures

Total Score	Your Grade
25+	A
22–24	B
20–21	C

Section III: Communication and Participation

Total Score	Your Grade
22+	A
19–21	B
16–20	C

Section IV: Support and Encouragement

Total Score	Your Grade
18+	A
16–17	B
14–15	C

Section V: Intergroup Relations

Total Score	Your Grade
18+	A
16–17	B
14–15	C

Section VI: Work and Productivity

Total Score	Your Grade
29+	A
25–28	B
22–24	C

Source: From *Creating Effective Teams*, by Sue Wheelan, © 2005, Sage Publications. Reproduced with permission of Sage Publications via Copyright Clearance Center.

Note what your strengths and development needs are. This is an exercise you might want to share with your own teams. Helping them learn how to be good group *members* will, in the end, make your job much easier and move the team to higher performance more quickly.

How Leaders Talk

Effective Communication

Even with the right style of leadership, managers are not guaranteed success. Clear communication will help all your interactions.

Consider that in any interaction you have the opportunity to be effective or ineffective (or somewhere in between) (see Figure 2.6). If you learn to select effective speech patterns, your message will be more successful.

For example, Figure 2.7 shows effective communication patterns, followed by ineffective patterns in Figure 2.8.

Ineffective   Effective

Figure 2.6 Communication effectiveness continuum.

Type of Communication	Example	Write Your Own
Praise Appreciate	You're on the right track. Thank you for you effort.	
Agree Support	You're right. I think you can do it.	
Probe Challenge	What are your goals? How can we do it better?	
Reflect Empathize	So you're saying that.... It seems that you feel....	
Coach Explain	I'd like to see more.... Here's how to do this....	
Delegate Collaborate	I'm turning this over to you. Together we can..	

Figure 2.7 Effective communication.

Type of Communication	Example
Order Lecture	You must... Do you realize that you..
Diagnose Moralize	What you need is... You really should...
Criticize Ridicule	You're not thinking straight. You ought to be ashamed.
Threaten Dispute	You had better... You can't do that...
Withdraw Patronize	Talk to me about it later. Just settle down.

Figure 2.8 Ineffective communication.

American Management Association
www.amanet.org

Tone of voice, body language, and the words you choose all contribute to the final message you send and your effectiveness as a leader. Effective communication patterns affirm and include as they help to build a positive relationship and allow you to influence and guide behavior of others. If you inadvertently choose an ineffective communication style, the result is that you exclude and create negative aspects in the relationship, which has consequences for your ability to lead. Increasing communication effectiveness is an ongoing challenge to leaders. There are times when special care needs to be taken to really do it well.

Challenges and Threats

If the organization faces threats or challenges, leaders talk realistically about problems, obstacles, and mistakes. But they do so in a way that promotes growth and improvement. Often employees can contribute to solutions and reframe the problem into an opportunity. When leaders withhold information, they create a workforce that is dependent rather than accountable. Many times someone closest to the problem sees the threat and can offer a solution that will open up new opportunities, for example, with customers.

Change

The goal of change requires leaders to discuss what needs to be altered, why it must be changed, how things will change, and who will be affected. Creating and managing change is one of the ways businesses grow. If there is no growth, eventually there is decline and death. To avoid negative changes, leaders should be proactive in soliciting ideas from their groups for change, listening to customer feedback, and driving change. In the long run this creates healthy organizations. Whether it is small changes to continuously improve or breakthrough changes to reframe the way business is done, leaders need to be effective change leaders.

When leaders talk about their vision, mission, or values, it is particularly important to make this communication as effective as possible. The leader is the compass for the group. As a leader, you are responsible for setting the direction and the goals of the group. Talk about the vision, mission, values, and goals should follow some specific guidelines.

Vision

Vision is future oriented. It's the leader's picture of the organization some time in the future. Most visions are three to five years out, but they can be less or more depending on the situation. Here leaders paint clear, concise, vivid, and inspiring pictures of what the organization can be and what steps they will take to get that picture.

Mission

A mission is the organization or group's basic purpose, its reason for being. Leaders describe what the organization must do day in and day out. They also show people how their work supports the attainment of the mission.

Values

Values are the things the leader believes and what is most important to a group or person. Leaders discuss the core principles that form the foundation for their actions, and they get followers to buy into and share values. They also recruit new people to the organization who are aligned to the company's values.

Goals

Goals are concrete steps to accomplish a group's mission. Some leaders refer to SMART goals—the Specific, Measurable, Attainable, Realistic, and Time-bound objectives they need to achieve. They talk about goals at the organizational, departmental, team, and individual level.

This following case will take you through one company's work to communicate its vision, mission, and values. This is taken directly from its website[4] and shows a nice example of the work a corporation needs to do to make its communications clear.

CASE C: Corporate Vision, Mission, and Values for RiskMetrics Group (RMG)

Originally founded upon a measurement of market risk in a portfolio, RiskMetrics Group is now the recognized standard in financial risk management. It extends its view of financial risk to include considerations in corporate governance, compliance, accounting, legal, transactional, environmental, and social risks. It is a proven leader in the disciplines of risk management, corporate governance, and financial research and analysis, and it is known for the ability to constantly innovate around these disciplines to address a broad spectrum of risk for financial institutions and corporations worldwide.

RMG Vision

"Change the World. Have Fun. Make Money. In that order."

Analyzing a Vision Statement

Visions are powerful when they

- Employ images that are clear, concise, and compelling.
- Express strong values and beliefs about the future.
- Focus discussion and shape choices about consequences.
- Challenge us to continually stretch beyond current performance.
- Create a picture of greatness for the future that the entire organization shares.
- Are treated as a corporate legend, both inside and outside the organization.

*Visions are most powerful when they are the true guide
for designing corporate strategy.*

════ S C E N E ════

RiskMetrics Group pursues its vision by keeping the original entrepreneurial style that allows for innovation and creativity from its employees. It has grown quickly and is a well-respected company because it promotes its stated values. It continues to grow by meeting competitors head to head, often providing expertise that others do not have. In addition to the vision, mission, and values, RiskMetrics is also guided by strategic imperatives and a long-term plan.

RMG Mission Statement/Purpose

"Simply stated, the purpose of RiskMetrics is to provide insight into a wide variety of financial exposures through research models and data, at our core we are a research company."[5]

Analyzing a Mission Statement

A mission statement is a written expression of the mission and purpose that serves as a guide for decision making and behavior.

Missions are powerful when they

- Employ language that is clear, concise, compelling.
- Express strong messages about the daily activities of the organization and its employees.
- Provide guidance for actions that must and/or must not be done.
- Express a purpose people can understand and support.
- Engage employees in devising creative ways to achieve the mission.
- Contribute to building an organizational culture that supports the company's vision.

*Missions are most powerful when they are visible
to employees and customers.*

SCENE

RiskMetrics now has twenty office locations that serve the world's financial centers. Clients come to RiskMetrics because of its expertise and its ability to evolve quickly in today's financial markets. Innovation labs are located throughout the world that explore new directions in the finance, technology, and market structures. Work in these labs includes a series of freely available technical documents, white papers, and market studies, as well as a significant number of new technology services that are rolled out to clients as part of a subscription business model. They also provide courses and educational programs to individuals and institutions for more in-depth training. Almost 40 percent of the company is focused on research and development.

RMG Values

"Living by our core values of *Respect, Ownership, Teamwork, Communication,* and *Client Focus* has been the most critical element in creating the vibrant and rewarding company that RiskMetrics Group is today. When practiced, these five values glue us together. While we are justifiably proud of our strong financial track record, the more enduring asset is the kind of company we've become. These values and success factors are deeply embedded and affect how we hire, how we work with and talk with each other, how we make decisions, how we develop and create our products, how we interact with our clients, and how we assess and reward individual performance."[6]

Respect
- Act with integrity.
- Demonstrate respect in all aspects of work life—treatment of co-workers, attitude toward clients, treatment of workspace.
- Accept and encourage differing views.
- Maintain and encourage a positive and fun work environment.

Ownership

- Be knowledgeable about overall business and ensure that direction is market driven.
- Take actions consistent with RiskMetrics Group values.
- Make appropriate choices about use of resources.
- Act on business opportunities that are not recognized by others, including those that are outside normal scope of role.
- Seek out those that will most benefit the company.

Teamwork

- Exchange ideas with others; help to cross train and educate others.
- Develop working relationships.
- Routinely seek opportunities to work on team projects, outside of assigned role.
- Work to resolve group conflict and boost group morale.

Communication

- Communicate in a clear, concise manner.
- Give and receive ongoing feedback.
- Be an effective listener.

Client Focus

- Be informed about developments in the industry and within the company.
- Anticipate, understand, and address the changing needs of clients by developing first-hand familiarity with client.
- Ensure client problems are addressed promptly and clients are satisfied.
- Work to retain clients and further strengthen client relationships.
- Provide opportunities for client input and feedback.

Analyzing Values Statement

Values are personal qualities or organizational practices that guide both organizational and employee behavior.

Values are most powerful when they

- Are values or characteristics whose definitions are easily agreed upon and recognizable in a person's behavior.

- Serve as a guide for daily behavior as well as strategic decision making.

- Are used to screen, interview, and hire potential employees.

- Are incorporated in the hiring process to the degree that they mold the organization in a way that helps it achieve its mission and vision.

- Are internalized by the people who work for the company.

- Become obvious to the customer who associates with the company's employees.

═══ S C E N E ═══

RiskMetrics Group has grown dramatically in recent years, yet it has stayed true to its entrepreneurial roots. With little in the way of corporate hierarchy, open communication and the giving and receiving of opinions are encouraged. Communication is open, and relationships with everyone are transparent. Every employee has the opportunity to get involved in a variety of initiatives. Surrounded by great minds and highly experienced industry experts, learning is an active part of life at RiskMetrics Group. It is well known for client focus and innovation.

Values are most powerful when they guide the hiring process and build a value-based culture designed to achieve the organizational mission and vision.

Company information used with permission of RiskMetrics Group.

Using Vision, Mission, and Values to Lead Others

While the example presented is for an entire organization, it is quite appropriate for divisions, departments, and even individuals to craft their own visions, missions, and values. Use the steps that follow to create a vision either for yourself or for the team you lead. The steps are a guide, not a recipe, so make the section serve your needs.

1. Create a vision of what you want to achieve.

    ■ What would you like to see in the future?

    ■ How can you improve or change the way things are done? What could be done better?

    ■ How would people be working together?

    ■ What kind of revenue would you generate (if you are in a revenue generating function)?

    ■ What would your relationships with customers look like?

    ■ What about service levels with customers?

Dream big at this stage. Later you can decide what's longer term and what is short term. You might want to mind map your first draft of a vision; some people prefer to talk it out with a colleague or friend, or just write ideas in a notebook. A mind map (see Figure 2.9) is a diagram used to represent ideas you have about the vision of the group or function. It is arranged with a radial around a central key word or idea, in this case "vision for..." Once you have the central idea, then you add ideas or concepts. Say you have a revenue target for the year that will go on a radial line; another line might be the word "teamwork," another, "work-family balance." As each radial line is added, other subtopics can be added underneath the main line. An example in Figure 2.9 is under "revenue target"—"outside the U.S. [number]" and "inside the U.S. [number]" have been included as lines branching from the main line.

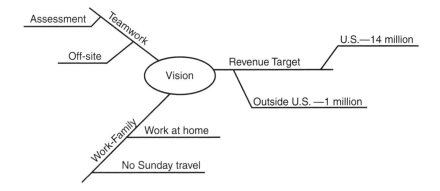

Figure 2.9 Mind map.

2. Once you have the first draft, look for things that you really want to accomplish over the next year or two. Save the other ideas for later.

3. Try it out on a friend. Use metaphors or visual language to help convey what you want the future to be. Refine it after your trial.

4. Communicate the vision to your team. When you are confident that you have the vision focused on what's important to you, think about how best to get the message out to your team. Be positive, use affirmative forms of expression, and talk about what you see happening. Experienced managers have learned that it takes saying things more than once to get the message out. Some leaders discuss goals in a meeting then send an email to recap those same goals; later, the manager might refer to the goals in a phone conversation or text message. In this way, the leader reinforces the message over and over until it takes hold.

5. Reevaluate your company's views and policies and write a final draft. In order to write a good vision and mission statement, begin with knowing what you and your organization stand for, understanding your values, what your customers want. Take some time to reflect and write a final draft of your vision, mission and values.

YOUR VISION, MISSION, AND VALUES

Use the space below to begin to work on your own vision statement. Start with your values.

Values:

_____

_____

_____

_____

Mission: The purpose of my team/function/group is to...

_____

_____

_____

_____

Vision: What I want for my team/function in the future is...

_____

_____

_____

_____

Remember that visions, goals, and mission can change, but a leader's values should remain constant to help develop a cohesive, trusting group.

▉ Career Enhancement Tool ▉
Scenario Planning

As a leader you must stay tuned to the changes in your world and make adjustments to them. One of the ways this can be done is through a process called scenario planning. This process involves looking at possible future scenarios for your business or group. Leaders need to anticipate and make adjustments for changes in the workplace, with customers, regulators, and the like. Scenario planning explores the impact that various drivers, such as societal changes, technology, economics, environmental changes, and political or regulatory forces have on your group or organization.

One of the hardest parts of the process is to play the role of facilitator rather than leader. This means you do not take a position in the discussion; rather, you gather information and record the ideas of others. During facilitation you should ask open-ended questions and monitor time and objectives of the meeting. Often it works to develop three scenarios: One suggests more of the same but better, one describes a worse outcome, and one suggests different fundamental changes to the scenario. This will require you to look at business trends and other data.

What do you know about the factors driving your group? As a leader you might note that interest rates are rising or that the workplace is more global. Once you identify the forces at work, it is time to compose your story. To develop a good story, look at what you actually believe. What you have overlooked? Is there something happening in your industry that could gain importance in the coming days or months? Scenario planning will help you prepare for the future. Leaders that practice this method are less often caught by surprise by changes in the markets.

American Management Association
www.amanet.org

What Is Your Leadership Brand?

Success is not final, failure not final: It is the courage to continue that counts.

—Winston Churchill

What's your favorite soda brand? Coke or Pepsi? Do you get disappointed when a restaurant only serves one or the other? Are you loyal to one or the other, or do you switch back and forth? Most people have brands that they consistently purchase because they are brand loyal. Once a customer is loyal to a brand, changing that brand loyalty is extremely difficult. Brands convey product identity and distinctiveness; people associate the brand with value or lack of value. Some people think of leadership image the same way they think of product brands in marketing. Brand managers work hard to get the right brand image known to customers. In a similar way, you need to manage your leadership brand. It won't do any good to be the best team leader in the company if no one knows who you are.

Your leadership image is determined by the way you act and are perceived by others. What is the appropriate image for a leader? How do you generate the appropriate image when taking charge? What type of image do you need to cultivate longer term? Why should you even concern yourself with these issues when it's results that ultimately matter? This chapter will help you understand the role of an appropriate leadership image and how to develop trust in your team. It will help make you more aware of how others see you and how you can manage the impressions that others have of you.

Perception Is Reality

Did you know that within 10 to 30 seconds people form lasting impressions of who you are? In an interesting study in schools, social psychologists found that once that first impression is set, it remains constant with little change over time. What the study did was ask a group of students to come into a classroom and rate a teacher they met for the first time. The ratings were consistent with those of other students that rated the same teacher after an entire semester.[1] This means that first impressions are critical in the business world.

There is a whole new field of study used by politicians and business executives alike called "impression management" where people learn to control the impression they give to other people. Just like an actor creates a character with the way he walks on stage, leaders must take charge of the image they send to colleagues and other business professionals. Here's a good place to start. Take the following assessment and find the current image you portray.

Step One: Assessment—What Is Your Image?

To what extent do you do the following?

1	2	3	4	5
Never	**Rarely**	**Sometimes**	**Often**	**Always**

The "Outer You"—Matters of Appearance

_____ 1. **Appearance.** Do you look like a confident, competent leader?

     _____ Good posture

     _____ Neat, clean, appropriate attire

     _____ Good grooming

_____ 2. **Eye Contact.** Do you make steady eye contact (without staring)?

_____ 3. **Smile.** Do you smile easily and naturally around people?

_____ 4. **Vocal Confidence.** Do you speak up clearly and confidently?

The "Inner You"—Matters of Character

_____ 5. **Friendliness.** Do you treat people in a friendly, accepting way?

_____ 6. **Precision.** Are you precise but relaxed when speaking?

_____ 7. **Enthusiasm.** Are you positive and enthusiastic, but not over-bearing?

_____ 8. **Attentive Listening.** Do you listen attentively to others?

_____ 9. **Smarts.** Are you up-to-date on the latest concepts and technology?

_____ 10. **Lack of Pretense.** Do you show your expertise without showing off?

_____ 11. **Genuine Concern.** Do you show genuine concern for others?

_____ 12. **Integrity.** Do you demonstrate high levels of integrity and honesty?

_____ 13. **Objectivity.** Are you fair, impartial, and objective in tough situations?

_____ 14. **Courtesy and Respect.** Do you show respect for others?

_____ 15. **Avoidance of Gossip.** Do you abstain from gossip and innuendo?

_____ 16. **Confidentiality.** Do you keep the secrets that others share with you?

Which areas do you need to further develop?

_____

_____

Interpretation: Your professional image is a function of the factors listed in the Image Profile. As much as 55 percent of the impression you make is visual; this means more than the old adage, "dress for success," because it also includes the nonverbal cues you give off with your body language. One image communication expert suggests you try to see yourself as others do.[2]

Have a friend videotape you when you practice a speech, or set up a camera and tape yourself walking into the room. It sounds strange but just like those old family movies, you will see things when you watch yourself that you never knew were there. All these things contribute to how effective, influential, and persuasive you are. Identify the areas where you scored lower: These are your opportunities for growth.

You can also talk to other people about your current image. Perhaps your manager could share what he or she believes your image is in the company. You can validate this assessment or alter it as necessary from the perceptions of the people who work with you.

Step Two: **What to Keep, What to Add**

Say that a leader does the self-assessment and then talks with a few other people. He has a list of four things rated high: technically smart, respectful, friendly, and keeps things confidential. Are there are other things he should add to increase his viability as a leader? Perhaps he could work on speaking confidently, since he would like to be able to voice his opinion more self-assuredly in meetings. He decides to work on that component of his image by taking opportunities to speak up in meetings. When this leader is done his image statement might look like this:

Technically Smart

Friendly Collaborator

Trustworthy and Respectful

Takes the Lead

Step Three: **Building the Brand Image**

You will need support to get your image known in the company. To do this, identify your personal board of directors (four to six individuals that can impact the building and perception of your image). Others have found it productive to look at work, within your professional relationships, and even among friends and family. Write the names of your "board" and review your rationale for selection of these individuals.

_____

_____

_____

Look at "Technically Smart" as an example of an image component. What can a leader do to continue to emphasize the perception of this component with others? Make a list as you brainstorm ideas. Would a more active role in the professional organization help you to build up the image as a technically sharp, cutting-edge professional? Or could you take an advanced course? The idea is to build on the strengths you already have.

_____

_____

_____

How to Change Negative Perceptions

Step One: Take Assessment.
Step Two: What to Keep, What to Add, AND <u>What to Lose</u>

This is a more difficult process. If people make an impression in the first 30 seconds and tend to keep it with little alteration a few months later, it stands to

---

═══ SCENE ═══

Andy is known as the office gossip. This will not build his leadership image, so he wants to lose that perception. How should he do this? What are the steps he needs to initiate? Who does he need to get behind him to make his plan work? Andy needs to develop a plan, review his plan with a "board" member, then stay disciplined and not get engaged in the gossip that goes around the office.

In this example, Andy could take a more direct approach and let the people know that he thinks it's not a good use of his time to talk about others. Or Andy could simply choose to leave the conversation when the gossip starts. The point is that he must actively disengage from his former pattern. It is a good plan to let others know in this kind of situation to help make the change. Perceptions are difficult to change, but adding support will speed up the process and hopefully keep him committed to change a habit that does not serve his career interests.

---

reason that changing an image is going to take work. Here is a scenario that will help you see what to do if you find yourself trying to change a negative image.

CASE A: Managing Image in a Difficult Situation

Here's a scenario where you will need to work through each step as if you are the leader in charge. Imagine that Tony's boss is transferring out of the organization and that someone outside the organization has been appointed to take over. This is the first time that the work group has seen Niles, so picture Tony and the new person, Niles, walking into a meeting of the work group. If you were Tony, what coaching would you give Niles to say and what would you tell him to do to make a positive first impression?

_____

_____

_____

What should Niles include in his inaugural address to this group?

_____

_____

_____

Some things you might consider are to counsel Niles to:

1. Show humility. _"It's an honor to have been selected...."_

2. Praise the group. _"I have been impressed with your...."_

3. Reaffirm the mission. _"I am 100% committed to the importance and successful accomplishment of our mission, which is to...."_

4. State your three most deeply held workplace values. _"Just so you know, I strongly believe in...."_ (State three values, such as teamwork, customer service, and integrity).

5. Ask for support. *"I look forward to working with you and am asking for your support in...."*

Of course, using examples of past successes or past effective behaviors will strengthen the first impression made in this sort of scenario.

Another challenge for leaders is a crisis situation. Imagine that you are back at work and that a major crisis has just erupted. To make matters worse, your boss has unexpectedly left the company. In the midst of this crisis, you have been picked to take over permanently. Picture yourself walking into a gathering of your work group. This is the first time that this group will learn that you are the new leader. They are in "near panic" because of the extraordinary crisis at hand.

How can you make a positive impression? What would you say?

_____

_____

_____

_____

Note: During a crisis situation, people expect a leader to take charge and do not expect to be asked their opinions. The crisis situation is not the same as day-to-day leadership.

Here are some things that would help you to build a positive leadership image:

- Look and sound confident.

- Act quickly and decisively.

- Express your confidence in the group.

- Set the example and lead through the emergency.

- Give instructions on what to do. Delegate specific actions.

- If you have a plan of action, announce it in a confident way, give specific instructions, and tell the group you expect them to follow your instructions.

- If you do not have a plan, ask for 5 minutes of input from the group, then make a clear decision on what should be done; give instructions and state that you expect people to carry them out.

Developing Trust

Trust is a cornerstone of good leadership every day, not just in a crisis. You need to look and sound credible, confident, competent, and caring. People need to trust you to get the best results. Trust is at the center of the leadership model in Chapter 1 for this reason. The ability to use all of the competencies in the leadership model and build the image you want to have hinge on the ability of others to trust you. Research on trust suggests that trust in management is linked strongly to innovation, productivity, retention, and engagement.[3] Trust can be like money, though, hard to get and easy to lose. When you develop trust with your team, here are some thoughts to keep in mind:

- **Credibility.** This is the belief that you have the skills to do the job, or competence that you need for a task. If you find you don't have the expertise, have the integrity to get help, ask for coaching. Take accountability for doing what you say you will do and get it done.

- **Trusting Others.** Leaders exhibit belief in the skills and abilities of others, and try not to be self-serving but rather focus their attention on the greater good of the person and the organization.

- **Openness.** This relates to predictability and the consistency between behavior and actions; it's not just speaking the truth, it's following through with actions.

Leaders become trustworthy through consistency in their behaviors over time. Trust develops in incremental fashion, so others will "test" a leader to see if he or she is reliable, and that will build or start to ruin the trust. Leaders should take the time early on to establish expectations for a group, which will start the process of building trust. It is critical for leaders to be deliberate and consistent in their dealings with their team when they are building trust.

Many times we are not aware that trust has slipped or been lost within the group or with an individual. The following Trust Check-Up will help you identify potential challenges with trust.

A TRUST CHECK-UP

To what extent do you do the following? Rate: Never, Occasionally, Often, Always

Credibility

1. As a leader, do you do what you say you will do?
2. Do you keep your technical skills up to date?
3. Do you take full accountability for actions? Do you notify others if you can't keep your commitments?
4. Do you say "no" if need be?
5. Do you have high ethical standards?

Openness

1. Are you open with others?
2. Are others open with you?
3. Do you communicate to appropriate people on the team?
4. Do you respond within 24 hours?
5. Do you use face to face or telephone for difficult conversations (not email)?

Trusting Others

1. Do you ask for help when it's needed?
2. Do you accepts apologies and forgive quickly?
3. Do you put conflicts "on the table"?
4. Do you give positive feedback to others?
5. Do you "watchdog" others to get tasks accomplished?

How did your assessment turn out? What are three trust strengths you exhibit?

- _____
- _____
- _____

Identify three areas where you can focus attention on building higher levels of trust in the future.

- _____
- _____
- _____

Think about what you have learned about trust. What lessons can you bring to leading your team in the present and in the future?

1. *Openness:*
   - Inform people honestly
   - Listen and respond to all concerns
2. *Credibility:*
   - Keep promises (Do what you say you will do)
   - Admit to unfulfilled promises
3. *Trusting Others:*
   - Acknowledge the expertise of others
   - Encourage the contributions of others
   - Build trust consistently

Building Trust: Virtual Teams

Virtual and remote leaders have an added challenge when it comes to earning trust. It seems that trust is even harder to gain virtually and much easier to lose. This is partly due to things like time delays, email, and lack of face-to-face conversations, but it can also be caused by cultural and language barriers. The group's productivity will be enhanced by working to increase trust. Trust starts with the relationship between team members. Researchers found that to facilitate trust in the first two weeks of a new group's existence, high-trusting teams spend a majority of their communications—whether emails or phone calls—communicating about non-task or social things.[4] They discussed things like families, hobbies, and the weather, rather than launching right into the project. This gives each member a chance to form some bonds before the work begins. In another finding, the members of the high-performing team always gave members a heads-up if something out of the ordinary was headed toward the team. They also made sure to give warning when they would not be on a particular call or correspondence due to travel, vacation, or other commitments.

This same study noticed that messages convey enthusiasm. In teams that had low trust, the messages that members exchanged revealed little or no optimism or enthusiasm. In the high-performing teams, there was excitement expressed about the project and references to other team members in comments like: "We are really starting to feel like a team. I can't wait to start on this project." There were members on the low-trust teams who showed little or no initiative; rather, the members waited to be told what to do while on the high-performance teams members volunteered for tasks.

The biggest issue that comes up in co-located, global, or virtual teams is that responses often take longer than people expect. If you are a leader on the East Coast of the United States and you send a message at the start of your business day in New York City to your colleague in Thailand, chances are you will not hear a response for at least 12 hours as your co-worker heads home for dinner and bed. One of the biggest differences in low- and high-performing teams is that feedback and responses are made as timely as possible and with quality responses—not just a "looks great," but a true analysis of the information. Finally, low-trust teams seem to spend a lot of their time on rules. Since enforcement is difficult, the team ends up bogged down in blaming one another for breeches to the arbitrary rules.

The high-performing teams used this sequence of communication:

- Social conversation
- Procedure but not rules
- Tasks

Working on Your Image over Time

Your leadership image will evolve. It should evolve in response to the different expectations you face at different times in your career. In the meantime, be intentional about what you want others to say about you. Remember to build and protect the trust. Work on the qualities you think are important to your career in a consistent manner and over time you will reach your goals. Here are some practice questions to focus your thoughts before you move on.

What examples can you give of the importance of trust in your workplace?

_____

_____

_____

What situations of mistrust have you encountered?

_____

_____

_____

What specific challenges do you have in terms of trust?

_____

_____

_____

■ Career Enhancement Tool ■
Feedback

It's the hardest thing to give to someone and probably the hardest thing to hear. But if you save all your feedback for the tough situations, you complicate your ability to lead. Instead, you should look for opportunities to give positive, corrective feedback. Leaders talk about current performance. They discuss what is going well and what needs to improve. They reinforce feedback to sustain good performance and give corrective feedback to improve substandard performance. Without constant feedback and information on performance, the individual and the group cannot expect to perform well. Feedback works best when you follow this simple rule: Ask first then tell.

═══ S C E N E ═══

Aidan's manager does not think he puts enough time into his graphic presentations. The result is that customers do not fully understand his products. Aidan and his manager stop for coffee on the way home from a joint sales call. The conversation goes like this:

"What do you think went well?" the manager asks Aidan.

"I think I held their attention well throughout the presentation, and they liked my sense of humor," Aidan says. Then the manager tells Aidan what he thinks went well. The manager might say, "I agree you had just the right amount of humor incorporated into your presentation. I also think you answered their questions well."

Then the manager asks, "What would you do differently next time?" Aidan answers, "Well, I think I lost them with my graphics. They were too complicated for their level of understanding." The manager then tells Aidan, "Precisely, I agree. The graphics did miss the boat. How do you plan to correct the confusion?"

In this example, the feedback is corrective, but it does not take a long coaching session to complete. Often managers think that feedback sessions will take too much time, so they "save up" their comments. This is less effective and can often lead employees to become defensive. If you can become a leader who provides consistent feedback, you will have stronger results. As a leader, you should not only give feedback, but you should seek feedback too. This will help get you out of a potential vacuum. Set up some time with your manager, trusted peers, or direct reports and ask them to tell you where they see your strengths and development needs. Even if you don't agree with them, you will know more about how you are perceived.

Leaders who put feedback at a low priority pay for it in the amount of time they spend redoing the work themselves, missing deadlines, or creating a stress-ful environments for everyone.

How Can You Build Influence and Power?

People are more easily led than driven.

—David Harold Fink
(medical doctor and author, 1894–1968)

If you ask someone to draw you a chart of who holds power in your organization, you will usually find that the chart looks very different from the company's organizational structure. This indicates that position and formal authority are not necessarily the highest sources of power. Many people think that position power will enable them to gain the influence they want to have. This is actually not the case. Influence and power are the energizing forces that get things done, and they are the indispensable tools of a leader.

Unfortunately, power often has a negative connotation. The word simply means the ability to overcome resistance and to get people to do things that they would not otherwise do; however, leaders, and especially women leaders, equate power with negatives. Whether you call it influence or power, you need it to lead. In this light, power should be thought of as the ability to energize people into action. The end goal is to develop a highly committed work force that is eager and willing to take on the challenges before them. The most powerful leaders align the self-interests of followers with the interests of the group, organization, or society so that transformation occurs. Leaders energize through four primary influence strategies:

1. **Inspiring:** This approach appeals to values and models the desired behavior.

2. **Negotiating:** The leader states what he or she wants, then bargains or exchanges to get to a win-win solution.

3. **Leveraging Relationships:** The leader uses friendships to influence others and builds alliances within the group or organization.

4. **Using Authority and Information:** This strategy includes the ability to appeal to logic and data to gain authority as an expert on a given subject. Often, with a strong and competent presentation of facts, the person can gain power.

Inspiring

Leaders who use this style are influential about ideals; leaders are able to shift followers from self-interest to interest in the greater good. For example, a soldier serves his or her country, and the leader motivates because of the person's ideals. It is not a new idea, as it is found in Homer's *Iliad,* that "He serves me most who serves his country best."[1] Leaders who strive for achievement as well as the greater good for group, organization, or society are found in all organizations, not just the military. The bottom line is that leaders are perceived as important to accomplish the group goal. How do leaders demonstrate going beyond self-interest for the good of the group? Here are a few ideas of what works to gain this kind of influence:

1. Talk about "the right thing to do" for the company or your group.

2. Jump in and help out when staff is short and the group is under pressure.

3. Give credit to the staff with upper management.

4. Be willing to make a personal sacrifice for the good of the group.

5. Walk the talk on values you support.

6. Make sure everyone understands the purpose of assigned tasks.

7. Be trustworthy—keep confidence.

Negotiating

Whenever you need the cooperation of another person to do something, however small, you are involved in a negotiation. Negotiations go on throughout your business day; the process involves trading of goods and services, favors and obligations. Whether you are in a discussion about lunch or interviewing for a job, you're involved in negotiation. Negotiation is making exchanges; it is the art of presenting your point of view and responding to the other sides in a way that encourages flexibility. Negotiation follows a predictable pattern. The first step of a successful negotiation is the right attitude. Some people think of it as "Let's Make a Deal," where the parties come together to find a solution. These people talk about "win-win" deals where both parties are satisfied with the results. This involves dialogue and mutual give-and-take, not a take-it-or-leave-it stance. Here is a four-step process for influencing someone you have no direct authority over:

1. Before you present your ideas, establish what you have of value to the other person and what he or she has that you want or need.

2. Ask questions to understand what the other person's interests are.

3. Only after you let others speak, present your request persuasively.

4. Always get commitment for what you want before you leave.

Establish Goals and What You Have of Value to the Other Person

- Exactly what do you want to achieve? Determine your goals.
- Identify what you can give that other person might want:
  - Resources: people, money, supplies, equipment, facilities
  - Information
  - Intangible rewards: goodwill, respect, supportiveness, understanding
- Develop your going-in strategy (hard or soft, open or closed).
- How much is it worth it to me to achieve this goal?

Remember that successful persuasion involves appealing to emotions as well as to facts and figures. How do you feel about the situation? How does the other party feel about the situation? Invest time in planning; you might even write a plan with someone you trust, and then modify it as the process unfolds.

Ask Questions to Understand What the Other Person's Interests Are

It is important to avoid launching right into a discussion of what you want. In fact, in some cultures this could be "business suicide." Any time you are involved in a negotiation, you should calmly use probing questions to determine what the other person wants or expects. Listen carefully to the other person to assess if she is ready, willing, and able to understand or accept your offer or proposal. If you sense you should wait, you probably should.

Remain nonjudgmental and keep your mind open to possibilities. Listen for pure content; don't interpret what is said to build a case that confirms your perception of the situation. Listen for facts. Your job at this juncture of the process is to understand the other side's position and then formulate a response to her point of view. Try to listen more than you talk. Your intention should be to get answers to specific questions that came up while you planned.

Present Your Ideas Persuasively

Once you have listened, you are ready to present your position and ideas persuasively. By this stage of negotiation, you know your audience, so discuss your understanding of his needs, desires, and expectations then show how your request, recommendation, or proposal can benefit by citing the unique strengths and advantages of your proposal. Try to align your position to something that you know the other person wants, too. You might say, for example, "I know that the company wants us to cut expenses this year and you have been looking for ways to do that. This project will cut expenses by...."

Avoid negative associations; rather, use testimonials, facts, statistics, evidence, and illustrations as well as other positive comparisons to prove your point. This will help you appeal to your audience's sense of reason and goodwill. If you have not convinced him, appeal to his curiosity or emotions and help him visualize success if he adopts your proposal.

Find out what you can about the personality of the other person. Is she likely to be impatient, accommodating, avoiding? You can adjust your style to hers. For example, with people who are apt to be impatient, try to prepare so that you can be brief. Why is the other party in this negotiation? How much personal interest does she have in your idea? Whatever the personality type, remember that information is power, so be organized with the data you need to influence and gain agreement to your idea.

Get Commitment for What You Want

Until you close with agreements and deadlines, you are not done. Explain what you want to accept, believe, do, avoid, or feel; be firm and assertive, but avoid power plays. You can ask directly for approval, acceptance, belief, or action in order to seek acceptance.

If you link the values and positive outcomes to the costs, for example, by suggesting a small experiment, you will have success. Link the value and positive outcomes of the decision to the costs. Make sure that you leave with both parties understanding the same agreement.

Leveraging Relationships

Negotiation is not the only way leaders can influence. One of the most powerful tools of influence at your disposal is your network. In today's flatter organizations, productivity and efficiency are enhanced with effective collaboration within and across functional, physical, and hierarchical boundaries. Finding relationships that add to your personal influence requires strategy and effort; once a team is in place, you can use this network as one of your power strategies. Here is a look at some of the people you might include in your network:

- Managers
- Customers/clients

- Friends/family
- College/former colleagues
- Vendors
- Colleagues/peers
- Lateral managers

Step One: Make a list of the people who are in your current network.

_____

_____

_____

_____

Step Two: Add targeted individuals to your list.

These individuals are the people you want to add to your network—the people who, if you knew them better, would potentially be able to increase your power and influence. For example, who delegates authority to you? Who decides what resources you have control over? To whom do you need access to achieve your own goals and objectives? Who could empower and expand your circle of influence? Add these people to your network list.

Step Three: Strategize to build relationships.

In order to make your network operate for you, it's important to build and develop relationships. This can be accomplished in a myriad of ways. You can get involved in interdepartmental projects or go to conferences or professional meetings to get to know others in your field. You can make presentations to different departments in your company or join a task force. Even simple things, like meeting for breakfast or lunch with members of your network, can help cement your relations. One key is to become more visible and available to your staff, peers, and senior management and encourage interdepartmental interaction. By seeking advice from others, listening and talking informally, you will grow your network.

One final thought on networking: Sometimes, the mere idea of adding one more thing to your day is overwhelming. In this case, consider this a longer term strategy. If your plate is too full, then consider when you might be able to add another person to your network and make a note in a calendar to call or connect with that person in nine months or next year at this time.

Using Authority and Information

Just as a network can help you develop as a leader, the way you use your authority and information will determine your ability to influence. Your technical expertise can be the influence you need to "sell" an idea. Don't underestimate the importance of your knowledge and competence as you use your technical expertise to "sell" an idea. If you are known as someone who is up-to-date and has good ideas, then leverage your reputation and image when you are influencing.

PRACTICING THE FOUR STYLES

Here's an opportunity to practice the four strategies of influence in this scene. You have just been named part of a committee planning the company picnic. Your task force has decided the picnic should be in a local park, not Central Park where it has been held in the past. The local park is smaller, not as beautiful, and has far fewer things to do, but this is the position you need to support. Write the approach you would take to influence the decision makers using each of the styles just discussed.

Inspiring _____

_____

_____

_____

Leveraging Relationships _____

_____

_____

_____

Negotiating _____

_____

_____

_____

Using Authority and Information _____

_____

_____

_____

Your answers could vary on this exercise; some possible solutions follow.

Your answer for inspiration could be centered on the idea that your company should be seen as supporting the local economy, helping the food vendors and people who would provide other services, such as recreation. The bigger "ideal" may be centered on what's best for the company, not just the picnic.

When you looked at leveraging the relationship, maybe you decided to elicit quotes from local vendors or community members. Or did you look to your own chairman, who has recently made reference to collaboration and support of the community as a corporate objective, which ties in with the local park as a venue?

When you thought about negotiating, what can you offer the folks who think Central Park is a better idea? You will need to do some research to see what would be of value to your company before offering anything. Maybe it is closer proximity to the office or less expensive. Here, remember to do preparation before making your case.

Finally, if you plan to use your authority and information to influence, you should provide data on the comparative cost, and maybe include the up side of building relationships in the community.

In this case, which of these styles do you think is the best choice to use? You can see benefits to each style. Could it be that you use a combination of two styles of influence? It will help you have the ability to use different styles in different situations. Here is an assessment that will help you identify the influence style you currently utilize.

SOURCES OF POWER AND INFLUENCE
Self-Assessment

Check the things that are your **highest** sources of power and influence.

1. My **Position**...the formal authority of my position, office, or title

2. My **Delegated Authority**...the specific authority delegated to me

3. My **Formal Rewards**...the tangible rewards I can give (money, awards)

4. My **Informal Rewards**...intangibles I can give (praise, attention, trust)

5. My **Formal Punishment**...things I can impose (firing, demotion)

6. My **Informal Punishment**...things I can deny (access, credit, time off)

7. My **Resources**...resources I can share or deny (money, people, data)

8. My **Performance Under Fire**...my crisis resolution and handling risks

9. My **Reputation**...my record for getting things done

10. My **Expertise**...my knowledge base, skills, and abilities

11. My **Political Savvy**...my awareness of and skill in political settings

12. My **Experience**...my experience base

13. My **Seniority**...my tenure in the organization or career field

14. My **Decisiveness**...my ability to make tough decisions

15. My **Personality**...my presence, self-confidence, image

16. My **Negotiation Skills**...my ability to inform and persuade

17. My **Communication**...of mission and purpose

18. My **Willpower**...my persistence, stamina, mental toughness

19. My **Access** to powerful people...my contacts with the powerful

20. My **Network**...my allies and supporters

21. My **Character**...my integrity, honesty, ethics, and moral standing

22. My **Good of the Organization**...my putting organization before my own self-interest

23. My **Values**...I walk the talk

24. My **Inspiration**...my ability to bring out the best in others

25. My **Authenticity**...as a leader

Which styles do you use to exert influence? (Note: 22 is part of two styles)
Inspiring: 15, 17, 18, 21, 22, 23, 24, 25
Leveraging Relationships: 9, 19, 20
Negotiating: 3, 4, 5, 6, 7, 8, 11, 14, 16, 22
Authority and Information: 1, 2, 10, 12, 13

_____

_____

_____

_____

_____

_____

Where do you see potential for developing other aspects of your power and influence? _____

_____

_____

Can you think of times you have used each of these styles? Do you overuse or underuse any of the styles? Think back over a situation that you wish had gone better. Would a different approach helped? Or maybe you didn't follow the process outlined earlier, especially the planning phase of negotiating. If you jump right into the negotiation without planning, you may find results less than you wanted them to be.

Increasing Influence Through Communication

Just as communication affects your image, it can affect your influence and increase your power. Remember from the communication effectiveness continuum in Chapter 2, repeated in Figure 4.1, that, for example, if you leave a meeting and say under your breath: "Well, that didn't go well!" then it's easy to see that this would fall toward the ineffective side of the continuum. On the other hand, while you dread a tough call to a sales representative, to your delight, when you hang up the phone, you say: "Wow, that was short and sweet, and she is going to adjust delivery charges." This conversation merits a check on the effective side of the log.

In Chapter 2, the communication was focused on building a positive leadership image. Now you want to look at these messages and determine how they help you build your influence and power. Just remember that any statement that starts with "you"—such as "You don't know what you are talking about." "You are not thinking straight."—and is meant to be corrective feedback is headed for the ineffective side of the chart. Patronizing, labeling, and withdrawing also are not destined to be effective strategies. Person-centered criticism is never effective. When you are trying to gain power, too many qualifiers water down your message before you gain understanding. Phrases such as "I could be wrong, but...," "I sort of...," "I am wondering if...," or "Maybe we could..." should be used sparingly when you are trying to gain influence.

Ineffective   Effective

Figure 4.1 Communication effectiveness continuum.

"Does that make sense?" or other questions added to the end of your statements makes the listener think you don't know what you are talking about, and this demeans your position.

Use short, to-the-point statements to increase effectiveness and gain influence. If the statement is effective, it will connect with the listener. Brief is definitely the best approach, but do not leave out specific supporting data. Here are some examples:

- "Great job" is made better by saying, "I am thrilled with your presentation to sales. Your graphics explained a very complicated issue, and as a result we landed the deal."
- Instead of "You don't take me seriously," say, "I want you to introduce me as the Manager of the Communications department, not as "our little genius.""
- Instead of "This phone does not get answered quickly enough," say "The phone needs to be answered by the third ring."

Being effective in influencing is not the same thing as being "right." Listen well to the other person's concerns and use open-ended prompts such as, "Tell me more about that." Consider whether the remark you are about to make will increase the other person's respect for you and further your goals before you speak. Will the words you want to say move you closer to a resolution? Or will it decrease overall effectiveness? Make sure that you know what you really want and be credible about what you say since it's your image and reputation at stake.

In review, to be effective:

- Be brief.
- Be specific.
- Say what you mean.
- Stay positive (not judgmental).
- Stay focused on your end goal.

Here's a situation for you to consider.

══ S C E N E ══

Sasha was asked by the president of the organization to lead a sensitive, urgent, and high-priority new initiative. This project will require at least five members of her staff of seven people full-time for the next thirty weeks. Sasha will actually need more people, resources, and help to meet all of her goals because of other commitments on her plate. The president told her that she could not hire more people or transfer people to her organization. She was also told to be creative and "get with the other managers for help."

Sasha sees that the project will require extensive expertise in information systems, which her team does not have. The best person in the organization to provide that kind of expertise is Mike, who works for another project leader, Gabriel. Sasha's initial estimate is that she will need Mike's type of expertise for at least three full days a week for the duration of this project. She suspects that Gabriel will balk at this request, but the president did say, "This project has top priority." Sasha has considered offering Gabriel credit and recognition in front of the president, as a way to influence him and get the loan of Mike's time.

Sasha's staff has told her that the six other members of Gabriel's department are not as skilled as Mike. Her staff mentioned that there is a former employee who trained Mike who is now an independent consultant and could probably help out on a subcontract basis. But Sasha has limited funds for consultants ($50,000 for the whole year). She figures that this person would cost at least $90,000 for three days a week for thirty weeks. Sasha has asked for the meeting with Gabriel to discuss providing help to her in the information systems area. She needs Mike's help. She sits down to prepare for this meeting.

1. What are her goals for the meeting?
2. What is her best possible outcome?
3. What is a minimally acceptable outcome?
4. What is an unacceptable outcome?

(continued)

(Continued)
5. What can she offer Gabriel to meet his needs?
6. What should her approach be in presenting her request? Hard or soft?
7. What should her approach be in sharing information? Open or closed?

Meanwhile, Gabriel reflects on the meeting as well. He suspects he will be asked by Sasha to provide IT support for the new project she has just been given. Beyond Gabriel's usual duties, he has responsibility for the organization's information system conversion over the next seven months, so he is reluctant to give up any of his staff. The executive vice president constantly inquires about the project; it's very important to him.

To complete this important conversion successfully, Gabriel estimates that he will need his best information system analyst, Mike, at least four days a week for the next twelve weeks, and then three days a week after that.

Gabriel figures that an option for Sasha is to hire a subcontractor. Melinda is an outstanding independent consultant who worked for him before she became an independent consultant and really knows her stuff. She is pretty pricey, her going rate is $1,200 a day, or $4,500 for a full five-day week.

He also has two new hires he could provide to Sasha. These two are smart, recent college graduates, and Gabriel could loan them to Sasha for her project. He suspects Sasha will balk at the suggestion of the new hires, but he could probably arrange a deal where they could be assisted by Melinda for a favorable rate ($800 a day). Melinda owes him a favor because of the excellent references and contact he provided her when she left. Another option that Gabriel thinks might work is to have Mike available for consultation on an occasional basis.

(continued)

(Continued)

Gabriel has worked hard to establish a good reputation in the organization. He realizes that he must succeed on the conversion project to be viable for future promotions. However, Gabriel also wants to appear to be a good team player by supporting Sasha's project while completing his mandate from the executive vice president to make the deadlines and budgets on the conversion. As he reflects on the meeting, he considers:

1. His goals for the meeting.
2. His best possible outcome.
3. An acceptable outcome.
4. An unacceptable outcome.
5. What his approach will be? Hard or soft?
6. What his approach will be in sharing information? Open or closed?

Do you think Sasha and Gabriel will leave the meeting feeling that it was a win-win? _____

Why or why not? _____

_____

What influence strategies are likely to play out in their conversation?

_____

_____

It is likely that all of them—inspiring, leveraging relationships, negotiating, and using authority and information—will be a part of this discussion, which will end in a win/win. There are enough resources to meet both leaders' goals in a timely manner. If they both start with respect for one another's significant challenges to meet deadlines and to maintain relationships, they will get off to a good start and close the meeting on the effective side of the continuum. It is important that both of the project leaders think about their needs and positions ahead of time.

Here are questions to ask yourself before meeting with someone you want to influence:

1. What is my goal?
2. What is my best possible outcome?
3. What is my least acceptable outcome?
4. What is unacceptable?
5. Who do I need to talk to (if anyone) to gain support for my idea?
6. What details and facts do I need to clarify?
7. What might be important to the other person?

In order to gain more influence, it is important that you understand the situation you are in and the best strategy to use when influencing others. Consider things like the key accountabilities, priority tasks, how the person is measured, how the person measures others, her career aspirations, her work and communication styles, the worries or areas of uncertainty in her job, as well as pressures from outside that could influence the discussion. If you try to draw on as many sources of power as possible, it is likely you will succeed.

■ Career Enhancement Tool ■
Intentional Storytelling

Leaders use stories to influence groups and individuals; the right story at the right time can change the way people understand the situation and react to it. Leaders may take some time to develop the ability to tell stories with intention, but the time is well spent. Intentional stories help get you where you want to go. Here's an example of intentional storytelling.

SCENE

Rob is a new manager with a group that has seen many layoffs, mergers, and acquisitions. The group does what it is told, but members are not energized by their work. Rob wants to change this dynamic. He decides to use a story to introduce the idea of increasing the level of team involvement. Rob says, "I coach community recreational football for 16-year-old boys in the town where I live. I played football. I watch football. I think I am a good coach. I know how to win. Game after game, however, we have lost. I have continued to work with the boys and believe that in one of these games their skills will come together and we will start to win.

"At a recent game, we were behind when one of the players came to me and said, 'Coach, put me in. I know how to win this game. I know I can do it.' I sent the kid back to the bench. I had plays I wanted to run, and the kid was not in my plan. We continued to lose, and the kid tried again. 'Coach, please put me in. I see what we need to do. I know I can do it.' At this point I thought the kid was persistent, but he was not going to change my plan. We continued to battle through the game. It's the last few minutes of the last quarter, and the kid tries one last time. This time I think I will teach him a lesson and put him in, since we will probably lose anyway. Well, I am sure you know what happened. The kid turned around the game and in the last few minutes our team scored not just one but two touchdowns and we won.

"So what did I learn? The people in the game usually know more about what's going on than I do. I have the title, but the kid saw the opportunities. As I stand before you, I want to tell you I know you know the way this business works better than I do. I want you to come and tell me when you see a play that needs to run differently. I will definitely give you the ball!"

The next time you need to move the ball, try some stories that teach or communicate your message and drive your vision.

How to Handle
Organizational Politics

One of the penalties for refusing to participate in politics is that you end up being governed by your inferiors.

—Plato

The definition of leadership suggests that the leader go beyond self-interest and think of what's best for the group or organization. Politics, on the other hand, is often thought of as doing things for personal gain. Politics is another word, like power, that almost always has negative connotations. How does politics fit into a definition of leadership that suggests the leader goes beyond self-interest? Is the word *politics* associated with negative behavior? What words come to mind? Write down several things:

_____, _____,

_____, _____,

Politics is viewed in a negative light by many leaders. Words like *favoritism*, *back-stabbing*, and *manipulation* are frequent examples of what comes to mind. This leads many to think the best solution is to stay out of politics. Office politics can cause a number of negative effects to the organization, not just your career. "Employees who feel frustration, guilt, shame, anger, humiliation and contempt on the job adopt defensive behaviors that end up reducing productivity," according to Henry A. Hornstein and Donald de Guerre.[1] Another study reports that women define success in the business world through values, corporate culture, and balance between work and family, while men define success by status, influence, profits, and market share.[2] Younger workers, Gen Ys or Millennials, enter the workplace with expectations for cultures that are supportive, open, and connected; they don't like conflict and negative political behavior.

So why not just avoid politics? Unfortunately, if politics is simply the use of strategies to gain power or influence, then it is essential that every organization or team has politics. Politics allows a leader to impact the corporate culture, the direct reports, and even the bottom line; so as a manager it is important to learn to manage politics. In fact, you can spend time on positive politics or work that improves your corporate culture and gain lasting benefits. The Gallup organization reports that the benefits of good corporate culture include "improved performance, profits and retention."[3] Employees engage and take a greater interest in their work when they are in tune with the politics of an organization. You may feel that you have no real control over the company culture, but every organization has subcultures, so at a minimum you can build a positive political culture within your group.

Over the last fifty years the cultures of most organizations have shifted from a top-down management paradigm to that of a more distributed leadership. Decisions made closer to the customer are faster and more effective because the data to make the decision is available to the people doing the work. With these shifts are changes in titles and organization structures. Recently, the CEO of a start-up said he purposefully did not use titles to designate power in his organization. Power comes from knowledge and expertise, not seniority or titles. This shift requires employees to form relationships and use their networks to accomplish things that are good for the organization; if they can accomplish this, they have used politics well. If instead they manipulate and leverage relationships to get their own agenda, they have used politics poorly.

When organizations engage in negative politics, they create organizational cultures with low trust where people withhold information, undermine one another, avoid responses to things like email, while spending a portion of their day working around the system. Conversely, politics with good intent leads to higher levels of trust and cooperation among employees.

====== **S C E N E** ======

Here is one story from someone who purposefully stayed out of politics. Cecille carefully avoided anything that looked at all political in her twenty-five years at the university. As an associate professor, she finally spoke with her Dean to find out why she had not been promoted in all those years. By now Cecille should really be at a full professor level.

The Dean noted that Cecille's student evaluations had been her biggest strength; she was a sought-after professor often invited by her former students to speak at their companies once they left the university. Unfortunately, among Cecille's peers, she was not seen as a leader. The Dean said that he was actually surprised that she even wanted to be viewed as a leader. After all, she had carefully orchestrated her career to focus only on teaching and not to get involved in the faculty/administration discussion about the future of the university. Occasionally, when pressured, Cecille had gone to meetings, but to avoid getting into heated discussions, she did not participate. Cecille was not perceived as a leader because she stayed out of politics. It had not occurred to her that she needed to learn how to participate, and no one had coached her to do so.

It is critical as you move from an individual contributor to a department or unit leader that you get involved in politics. As a leader, you represent a group, and you no longer represent just yourself. Therefore, your political skills become an important component of your job. Don't sit back like Cecille and think you are managing politics, and do not wait twenty-five years like Cecille to ask for feedback!

The Positives of Politics

As a leader, you should have several reasons for using politics in your organization:

- **Achieving the organization's mission:** Managing your resources and human resources to achieve the organizational mission and objectives.

- **Procuring needed resources:** Making sure your team has the resources it needs to achieve those objectives.

- **Protecting your constituents:** Doing all you personally can to ensure your group's success and guarding against failure.

- **Rewarding your constituencies:** Ensuring their efforts are justly rewarded.

- **Ensuring goodwill and respect:** Making your group's achievements known so they get the recognition and benefits they deserve.

As you work to fulfill your responsibilities to those you lead you must participate in politics. So the next question is, How do you participate in politics?

POLITICAL SKILLS SELF-ASSESSMENT

To what extent do you....

1. get impatient with political process and make procedural errors?

    Always   **Sometimes**   **Never**

2. discredit the ideas, efforts, or accomplishments of others?

    Always   **Sometimes**   **Never**

3. make end runs around the boss because you feel it's necessary?

    Always   **Sometimes**   **Never**

4. burn bridges?

    Always   **Sometimes**   **Never**

5. challenge the boss's strongly held beliefs?

    Always   **Sometimes**   **Never**

6. criticize peers and others after meetings end and when they are not present?

    Always   **Sometimes**   **Never**

7. fail to anticipate consequences of your actions well?

   Always   **Sometimes**   **Never**

8. complain about your boss or upper management?

   Always   **Sometimes**   **Never**

9. give advice that is meant only to serve personal interests?

   Always   **Sometimes**   **Never**

10. subtly cut out of events, meetings, decisions, or plans?

   Always   **Sometimes**   **Never**

11. create partnerships with powerful people?

   Always   **Sometimes**   **Never**

12. defend your rights, interests, needs, and resources directly and assertively?

   Always   **Sometimes**   **Never**

13. negotiate, compromise, or even withdraw when appropriate?

   Always   **Sometimes**   **Never**

14. believe corporate politics are a necessary part of organizational life and work to adjust to that reality?

   Always   **Sometimes**   **Never**

15. anticipate where the land mines are and plan your approach accordingly?

   Always   **Sometimes**   **Never**

16. tell others what they are expecting to hear rather than what you know to be true?

   Always   **Sometimes**   **Never**

If you think you had too many answers "always" to the negative questions in the self-assessment (questions 1-10 and number 16) and you want to be a leader, it is time to shift some behaviors.

American Management Association
www.amanet.org

How Do You Learn Political Skills?

Organizations are politically complex and to maneuver through them takes a multifaceted approach. One way is to observe people who do it well. Another is to ask your mentor to help you understand things you need to know. Obviously, stop doing any of the negative behaviors you identified in the Political Skills Self-Assessment.

Make sure you are clear about your own integrity and your core values. One manager says that being honest and demonstrating integrity and respect in all he does is core to his leadership approach. It makes decision making easy when you have a view on how you will play politics.

Continue to work on your image. People differ in the impressions they make with others. People who have a positive impression get more things done through the organization than those who are not liked or leave negative impressions. Ask others for feedback about how you come across during meetings and times when you are attempting to influence a group; increase your ability to be self-aware.

Another part of being politically astute is anticipating how ideas will be received. Even if you do everything correctly, there will be times when you have to protect yourself or your group from the manipulations of others. There are five ways that you can increase effectiveness in these situations.

1. Watch for and protect against the devious political tactics of others.
2. Avoid making political blunders.
3. Create partnerships with powerful people.
4. Defend your rights, interests, needs, and resources assertively.
5. Negotiate, compromise, or even withdraw when appropriate.

How to Win at Politics

As a leader, you need to manage the political climate in your team. The culture in your group could include such things as openness and partnership; it could refuse to tolerate any of the negative political behaviors. As a member of the management team, you need to encourage the political climate and help transform your team as well. Team members today have a different role, too. In the past, most important decisions could be made by management. Today team members are called on to identify problems, think of solutions, create and implement changes, and develop innovations.

- Pinpoint what you want and why.
- Identify who controls what you need.
- Find out who can help you get what you need.
- Decide what you need to do to get what you need.
- Go for it with determination and resolve.
- Watch out for the harmful politics of others as you go.
- Protect yourself as you go.

Part of your role is to encourage team members to be proactive and take charge. Team members need to buy into their role in creating culture. One technique is to make a chart like the one shown in Figure 5.1, then share it with your team.

This?	Or This?
I do my work well and mind my own business.	We pull together so we can all win.
It's not my problem—let management fix it.	It's better to jump in and get this resolved.
I'm not getting involved in conflict.	Let's work it through and resolve our differences.
I'm not giving anyone feedback, especially my manager.	How can we improve if we don't give feedback?

Figure 5.1 Proactive chart.

American Management Association
www.amanet.org

Create your own chart with negative attitudes and choices in one column and the behaviors you want to encourage in a second column. Have a group discussion and agree to a personal team list. Here are some suggestions to consider for the positive side of the chart:

- We give and receive feedback.
- We keep the needs of the organization in focus.
- We look for ways to make things better here, to innovate.
- We share our skills and expertise with colleagues.
- We maintain a positive attitude within the group.
- We have many voices inside the team, one voice outside.
- We demonstrate leadership within the team.
- We handle task conflicts immediately.
- We avoid personal conflict and seek solutions.
- We communicate information that others need, returning emails promptly (within 24 hours).
- We use email for short, task-related communication.
- We keep meetings short and to the point, have agendas with outcomes listed, and send the agenda out at least the day before the meeting so that others can prepare. A summary is made of our meetings.
- We develop team rules for our meetings, things like one conversation at a time, starting and ending on time.
- We work on building relationships within the team.

Add to this list as you see fit; delete what doesn't make sense for your group. The idea is to create the framework that will drive the culture you and the team want to create. Good cultures are not an accident; they are created and maintained by the group and its leader.

How decision making gets done in organizations is often reflective of the culture. There are at least four choices for the level of empowerment that you want the group to have. Each is appropriate in some situation. They are directly aligned to the leadership styles in Chapter 2.

- **Stage One Leaders:** Leaders decide without consultation with employees, they inform employees, who comply.

- **Stage Two Leaders:** Leaders make decisions, but get employee input first, then inform employees, who comply.

- **Stage Three Leaders:** Team members make decisions and recommend a course of action, but must seek approval from manager before acting.

- **Stage Four Leaders:** Team members are given full authority to make decisions, create action steps, and implement without any further approvals from management.

Think about the consequences to culture with each of these levels of decision making. If all decisions are made with a Stage One leader style, what would the culture look like? When is it a best choice of a style? For example, Stage One style is appropriate if the information is sensitive, team members lack skills or experience, and accountability can't be shared. Overuse of this style can create a very dependent culture.

At Stage Two, management may feel unable to share accountability for the decision, but they do want input from the team. This decreases dependency somewhat, but still creates a dependent culture.

At Stage Three, active participation is desired, but risk is high or the team is still lacks experience to make decisions alone. If this style is only used when risks are high or the leader feels the team is not experienced enough to make the decisions, the team will move toward Stage Four.

If a team has been together for some time and establishes a proven track record, it needs to be able to make most (about 60 percent) of its decisions at Stage Four. If this doesn't happen and the team needs to get approval for everything, then team work gets bogged down, innovations won't take place, and the team will be hampered in responding quickly to customer needs. The culture becomes demotivating and risk averse. However, the team may need to learn to make decisions as a group. There are three choices for members to consider:

- Majority rules: Decision with the most votes wins.

- Consensus: Agreement when everyone can work with or buy into the decision.

- One member decides: Person with the most expertise, experience, or ownership decides.

Figure 5.2 shows the picture of decision-making styles added to the Leader Styles chart. Note how the direction is from controlling to empowering.

One of the critical jobs of a good leader is to manage politics. Randy Williams, Managing Director of Redmond Williams (RWA), a firm that helps enhance compliance, governance, and issue escalation in corporations, reinforces that a mentor with a proven political track record is essential. In fact, in the 2008 Institute for Corporate Productivity and American Management Association study[4] that Ms. Williams helped author, mentoring programs for new hires received the highest correlation between the cultural index and market performance. However, as Ms. Williams notes, only 17 percent of the respondents use mentor practices. This is an area for potential development in most organizations that can lead to improved cultures very quickly. This suggestion keeps appearing from different sources because this might be the simplest way to effect a positive change in your corporation or team.

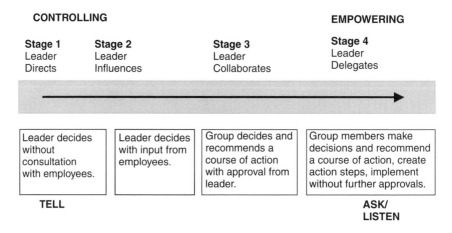

Figure 5.2 Decision-making styles with leader styles chart.

▪ Career Enhancement Tool ▪
Avoiding Political Blunders

The opportunity for political blunders is particularly high when you transition to a new job. This is a time when everyone watches you to see how you manage the new role. Some of you will be fortunate to have managers who are good coaches; others will not. One way to avoid the blunders is to prepare yourself for the transition into the new job. Do your homework!

In a new position, leaders focus on what they need to accomplish in their new job, what results are expected of them, who is on their team, and what are their skills. They likely focus on the culture of the organization before accepting the job and may note the ways work gets done and the corporate values. The thing that no one talks about is the politics. If leaders are lucky, they won't stumble into this problem. However, many leaders do innocently fall into situations. It's like traveling in a foreign country; if you don't understand the culture, you can inadvertently make mistakes.

════ SCENE ════

Risa just started as a manager in the training department of a research lab. Engineers and scientists work on very exciting things in this lab, technology that will someday change the way work is done. She jumps into the job with youthful enthusiasm. In her first management training program, an experienced senior manager challenges her on the material she presents. He thinks it's very academic and won't help him on the job. In Risa's prior jobs, she was empowered to challenge back; open discourse was valued. So she jumps in to make her point. Later, she finds out that the perception of the group is that she is overly aggressive, doesn't listen well, and didn't respect the position of the participant. She is shocked. What could Risa have done to be better prepared for her first foray into presenting training materials to this audience?

American Management Association
www.amanet.org

Before your first day as leader:

- Make it your goal to learn how things are really done in your organization.
- Find out how your boss likes work to be done: email, written report, talked through. What works for the boss?
- Make sure you understand your boss's priorities and goals.
- Align your goals and priorities with those above you.
- Assess your staff.
- Address problems quickly.
- Assess the real leaders in your group.

As you transition into the organization over the first six months:

- Actively learn more about the organization and the people in it.
- Get to know everyone personally.
- Travel to other locations.
- Build relationships with all stakeholders outside your immediate team.
- Pay attention to challenges to your leadership, remember Chapter 2 and see it as "good" conflict, but do address it.
- Don't make any big changes until you really understand the organization.
- Build trust with others (see Chapter 3).
- Use this as a time to establish who you are and tell people what you value.
- Talk to your group about stages of group development and your vision for an empowered team.

Risa now understood that in this organization a better way to handle the challenge would be to ask a simple question after the Director challenged the content. She might say, "What do the rest of you think?" A more facilitative approach, rather than challenging, would have been more in keeping with the culture. Fortunately, one blunder in the first week on the job does not end a career, but to avoid the situation in the first place is the goal. Get off to a good start by understanding the real power structure in the organization.

American Management Association
www.amanet.org

How to Motivate People

A competent leader can get efficient service from poor troops, while on the contrary, an incapable leader can demoralize the best of troops.
—General of the Armies John J. Pershing

In the best groups, employees will do more than they originally thought possible. A good leader's long-range goal is to create the culture where employees can reach their full potential. In Chapter 1 the leadership model that was introduced showed motivation as one of the four key clusters of behaviors ascribed to a leader. For individuals to give leaders their best work, they need to feel that the leader truly wants the best for them as individuals. To get the best results from individuals and groups, leaders must build self-confidence and commitment in employees. One way to do this is through inspiration and motivation. Over the past fifty-five years, there have been numerous surveys on what motivates employees to do their best work. Unfortunately, the biggest finding overall is that what motivates people is different person to person because there are personal and situational factors that change motivators. However, a few principles have been found to be true for everyone:

- People repeat what is positively reinforced.
- Immediate feedback is best.
- Incentives work best.

Employees enter organizations with expectations of their employers. In an article in *The Health Care Manager,* Charles McConnell reports that workers come with a set of expectations. Some of the expectations that relate to motivation include that "leaders can be respected and admired; employees will receive fair treatment from colleagues in a safe work environment; the organization will recognize individual efforts, or good performance as well as fair monetary compensation."[1]

Generations at Work

One motivational issue is a multigenerational work force. Examples of generational differences crop up every day in the workplace. Do you wonder why your 50-something co-workers spend time on phone calls with clients when a text message or an email would handle the issue more quickly? Generational tensions are at an all-time high and, with four generations in the workforce, only stand to go higher. This latest diversity issue impacts all areas of the workplace, especially employee motivation.

To understand a generation, leaders need to look at what was happening when an employee came of age—what shaped an employee's values. Is the employee a product of the baby boom, arriving after World War II to parents hoping to provide a better life by indulging their children? If so, she might be a workaholic who looks for her workplace to recognize her importance to the organization while she struggles not to burn out? Did the employee grow during the struggling economy of the 1970s, worrying about shortages of natural resources and lack of good jobs? Maybe a Gen Xer who "works to live" is the result. While these are broad generalizations, they can impact an employee's work habits.

The different generations bring their unique backgrounds to the job. This is not to say that leaders need to become workplace therapists by helping each generation deal with its baggage, or is it to say that generalities about each cohort hold true for all employees. But by looking at each generation broadly, leaders can more effectively manage.

For example, some Gen Xers see Boomers as dictatorial and workaholics. It is not in their experience to place work above their family. On the other hand, Boomers look at Gen Xers and see them as lazy and lacking in a work ethic—after all, who walks out at 5:00 when there is still work to do? These are important generalities as you work to motivate a multigenerational group.

Here are some suggestions for dealing with generational diversity:

- Identify your own opinions and stereotypes about the different generations.
- Increase your knowledge of generational differences.
- Receive feedback in order to identify strengths and areas for development.
- Interrupt your own stereotypes by looking for different interpretations of the information.
- Receive generational training.

You also need to pay attention to individual and group energy level. How do you influence motivation? There are four tried-and-true ways: Know your people, provide positive feedback, use inspirational and motivational language when communicating, and use behaviors that motivate.

Know Your People

There is no better way for a leader to understand motivation for another than to get to know that person as an individual and understand what is important to each of them. Employees will vary in their beliefs about what they can accomplish. This will affect their efforts, which in turn affects their results. Learning your employees' needs, and how they pursue the fulfillment of those needs, will help you provide the right motivation and feedback for each person.

MOTIVATION ANALYSIS

Rank order (1 = high) the <u>five outcomes</u> that you think are most important to this employee at this time. In the second column, check the outcomes you feel your direct report would say are lacking in his or her job. Circle the ones you have control over or can provide.

	Importance Rank	Lacking in Job
1. Clear assignments, expectations, goals	————	————
2. Meaningful, challenging work	————	————
3. Opportunities for growth and advancement	————	————
4. Opportunities for teamwork, input, and belonging	————	————
5. Opportunities for initiative, creativity, judgment	————	————
6. Prompt feedback, recognition, appreciation for work	————	————
7. Rewards that provide something of value for good work	————	————
8. Clear accountability and consequences for performance	————	————
9. Consideration for people's needs, desires, likes, and dislikes	————	————
10. Time, resources, support, training to be successful.	————	————
11. Other? _____		

You can complete one of these forms for each person in your group, or, alternatively, you can ask each person to complete the analysis and then follow up with a meeting to discuss actions you jointly can take to maximize motivation for each employee.

Provide Positive Feedback

Over the past decade, scientists have explored the impact of positive-to-negative interaction ratios in work and personal life; they found that this ratio can be used to predict—with remarkable accuracy—everything from workplace performance to divorce. This work began with noted psychologist John Gottman's exploration of positive-to-negative ratios in marriages.[2] Using a 5:1 ratio, which Gottman dubbed "the magic ratio," he and his colleagues predicted whether 700 newlywed couples would stay together or divorce by scoring their positive and negative interactions in one 15-minute conversation between each husband and wife. Ten years later, the follow-up revealed that they had predicted divorce with 94 perent accuracy.

Barbara Fredrickson, a psychologist, and mathematician Marcel Losada found that work teams with a positive-to-negative ratio greater than 3:1 were significantly more productive than workgroups that did not reach this ratio.[3] (There is an upper limit to positive to negative ratios–it's 11:1—after that work groups worsen!)

When leaders display positive emotions, others take note and apparently take action as well. For more information on how to increase positive emotions at work read Tom Roth's *How Full Is Your Bucket?*,[4] a book that draws on decades of research to show leaders how to increase positive emotions at work.

Use Inspirational, Motivational Language When Communicating

Leaders have the opportunity to provide motivation through their choice of language. The head of national Marketing and Sales gives these two speeches to his reports gathered to hear their business results for their first year. Contrast the impact of these messages.

Talk One:

Our numbers exceeded our projections so now we are a viable resource to the corporation. Thank you for your work.

Talk Two:

Two years ago, when the federal regulations and managed care exerted tremendous pressure on our industry, you folks were brought in to offer a new way to sell our products. We knew you would succeed, but no one expected that it would happen so overwhelmingly or so quickly. Our reputation with customers is better than any of our competitors, our sales figures are incredible, and you already have identified new ways to leverage our business in the

future. An increase of about $7 million from last year's budget shows the con-
fidence management has in this division. I am confident your success will
continue.

What do you notice about the two talks?
Can you see how you can adapt your talks to be more motivational?

Use Behaviors That Motivate

Language motivates, but so do actions. Let your behavior show that you recognize effort through things like informal celebrations after the completion of
difficult projects. You can send a note or email to senior personnel that high-
lights the accomplishments of a team or simply commends associates in another
department for a job well done. Remember that an old-fashioned handwritten note can motivate because it is so rare to receive in today's work world.
While words are strong motivators, actions offer incentives for highly motivated
associates go even further to distinguish efforts.

══ SCENE ══

When Jack Welch was CEO of General Electric, during the late
1980s, GE purchased RCA in the process of merging the two companies. The GE corporate data center needed to be moved from Sch-
enectady, NY, to Cherry Hill, NJ, where the RCA corporate center
was located. This process involved relocating families, layoffs, downsizing, and many anomalies such as differing pay scales for people
working side by side. Morale plummeted as time extended into more
months than expected. Every month, the senior teams met in Fairfield,
CT, to go over progress on the project. Most of the time the results of
the meetings were further staff cuts.

A Human Resource person in Cherry Hill was quite concerned
about further cuts and sinking morale. Jack Welch was known as
"neutron Jack" in those days for "blowing up" the company with

(continued)

(Continued)

many layoffs and closed businesses. There was a sense of fear in the culture that anyone could be next. About the time things were really bad, this HR manager was introduced to Jack Welch at a corporate training program. Jack, seeing her name tag said *HR Corporate Information Technology*, said, "How are things going with the merging of the data centers?" She briefly considered how to answer him and then said, "Well, frankly, Jack, I am getting worried about the group; they work weekends and often very late at night." Jack's response shocked her. He said, "Well, you are the HR person, you should do something about it!" Caught completely off guard with his response, she replied, "Now, really Jack, who do you think they listen to, me or you?" Someone else entered the conversation and it ended there.

Playing it back in her mind the rest of the night she realized how flippant she sounded. She wondered if she would lose her job. Imagine how this manager felt when she received this handwritten note from Jack Welch below.

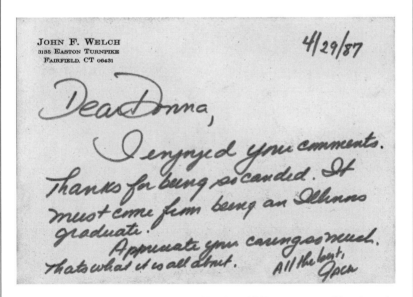

Figure 6.1 Thank you from Jack Welch to H.R. manager. (Reprinted with permission from John F. Welsh)

"Appreciate your caring so much." Amazing what a lesson this is in reinforcing behavior you want to encourage!

The point in sharing the note is the power of a handwritten note. We use email so much today that this note is framed and on the wall in this former HR person's office to remind her of the importance of being candid and caring enough to speak up, even to Jack Welch, and to encourage her as a leader to take the time to send a personal note.

Even if you do everything "right," you are likely to have times when things just don't work. Some situations are more challenging, and some people are more challenging. Here's a look at what to do with some of the difficult situations you might face.

People Who Resist Your Authority

Imagine that you have been selected to take charge of your current work unit. How do you expect your former peers will react to you during your first day in charge and for the first few weeks and months? What might resistance look like? For some people resistance is aggressive, others will be passive aggressive; in either case, you need to deal with it as soon as possible. Expect early tests of your authority and plan to meet them by being firm and fair. If you don't establish limits early, you will live to regret it. If you think the people in question are never going to accept the situation, then you have to find a way to move them out of your organization.

When you notice resistance, you need to decide how you want to address it immediately. A direct conversation with the person is likely to be the best approach. You might say: "How are you feeling about my promotion?" Focus on feelings, try to show support regardless of whether you agree. After the employee has had his or her say, you should state your position, "I can understand how you feel, but here's the thing, it wasn't my decision, and I need you to be a fully participating member of the team...." If you can add things that you value about the person's work in this conversation, that's helpful. You can ask if there is anything you can do to make the transition work better for the person.

Be as responsive as you can in a first conversation. If there is a repeat of negative behavior and you need to have a second conversation, you will need to be clear that the inappropriate behavior should stop. Talking with someone in your Human Resources department to get advice is always a good idea. HR people will have lots of experience and know how the company likes these situations to be handled. Some of these situations resolve themselves because the people find work in other departments and transfer, or they leave the company. If this is a person who is a personal friend and whom you have shared work experiences with, your new role may mean you have to limit some kinds of information sharing. You need to consider your role as a representative of management and as a leader in the organization; keep confidential the things that would be inappropriate to share. It will help your former peers manage a new definition of your roles if you are consistent in doing this.

Other Difficult Situations

There are many other difficult situations you may have to face, including layoffs, addressing poor performance, behavior problems, confronting sexual harassment, changing work spaces to a less desirable location, or turning down a request for a promotion.

Whatever the situation, there are some basics you can use to plan for handling them:

1. Plan for the conversation, even to the extent that you role-play with a friend if it will help you feel more comfortable.

2. Get company advice from HR about polices and past practices. How have these things been handled in the past? Always make sure you have the right time and place to conduct the conversation privately and without interruption.

3. Make sure you stay focused and don't react emotionally to the employee's or boss's attacks if they occur. Be direct; bring things out in the open.

Handling Difficult People

We are all difficult for someone at some point in our lives. For example, in a proposed layoff, it is predictable that people will be difficult; emotions will surface, making conversation more challenging. Those kinds of situations may be difficult, but they are at least understandable. When we are difficult to others, it can come from a variety of places:

- Self-image
- Values
- Desires
- Attitudes
- Needs
- Beliefs
- Experiences
- Interpretations we make of other's behavior

In some instances, the catalyst for difficult behavior is external. Sometimes our own behavior provokes the other person or enables bad behavior to continue. It could be a personality clash, our leadership style, or the way we communicate. The only way to know for sure is to move beyond the behavior and connect with the person one-on-one. You must maintain a careful balance between finding out enough to resolve your difficulties with the person and becoming an amateur psychologist.

Here are five typical difficult people to handle. Decide what you would do for each of them.

The Staller

Joe holds up everybody and everything. You are trying to lead your group to completion of a major project, but Joe keeps asking you to delay the deadline. His group has nicknamed Joe The Staller. How can you discover what the problem is and get Joe to act?

Tips for Handling the Staller

- Help get the true conflicts to the surface.
- Tell him you appreciate his thoughtfulness, but timelines are equally important.
- Work together to problem solve.
- Work out a win-win solution.
- Support the decision.
- Ask for timelines.

The Emotional Hothead

Lauren is a member of your group who is typically a good performer. The problem with Lauren is that she blows up at you and other team members when things don't go her way. When you asked Lauren for a status update on a major client project, she stormed out of your office. How can you effectively deal with Lauren?

Tips for Handling the Emotional Hothead

- Remain outwardly calm, even if Lauren is not.
- Suggest you talk tomorrow or later in the day when she has cooled off.
- Listen.
- Practice reflective listening and summarize what you have heard her say.
- Use phrases such as: "I disagree, but tell me more," "I want to hear what you have to say. Please listen to me, too."
- Show support. Tell Lauren that you appreciate how strongly she feels and say you want to use some that emotional energy constructively, to help solve the problem at hand.
- Indicate areas where you agree; discuss areas where you disagree.
- Ask for solutions/input; brainstorm solutions together.

The Complainer

Ivan complains about everything. He doesn't like the layout of the office space and often complains about the way his co-workers design programs. He has just complained about the way you handled a department meeting. What strategy should you use to turn Ivan into a problem-solver rather than a problem-seeker?

Tips for Handling the Complainer

- Don't be defensive.
- Listen and acknowledge. Don't argue.
- Don't agree or apologize.
- Ask questions.
- Explore or suggest possible alternatives.
- Encourage him to share in problem resolution and implementation.

The Backstabber

Nora, your fellow sales manager, is very friendly and helpful when you are together. You recently voiced some concerns to Nora privately about your group's customer service. You have just heard that Nora complained to your boss about your management style and your direct reports' lack of customer service skills. Apparently, this is not the first time she has complained about you. You feel like you have just been stabbed in the back. How will you approach Nora?

Tips for Handling the Backstabber

- Address the behavior openly.
- Remain calm, but discuss your thoughts about blaming.
- Probe for reasons for backstabbing behavior.
- Discuss solutions for moving beyond backstabbing.
- Address each instance until it stops.

Mr. Perfect

Peter thinks he knows it all. Whenever you try to offer tips on how utilize more effective e-solutions, Peter claims he knows best. He is very bright, keeps up-to-date with this field, and is a good performer. However, many field experts have told you your group needs to change technologies, and in Peter's perfect world the current technology is the best. How can you convince Peter otherwise?

Tips for Handling Mr. Perfect

- Be well prepared.
- Listen and paraphrase what he says.
- Don't challenge/ask questions to lead him to see his errors.
- Praise his ability.
- Focus on the solution.

Changing Your Interactions with Difficult People

What other difficult people do you have to work with? You can't change a difficult person's personality, but you can change the interaction between you. This puts you in control of the situation. If you change your own behavior, it often leads to a change in the other person's behavior. Remember that the difficulty is often a symptom rather than the cause of behavior.

Here are some ways you can change your own behavior when dealing with difficult people:

- Try to absorb what the difficult person is saying and try to get his or her point of view. When you listen, try not to react, but rather look within to your true feelings. Ask yourself: Why does this behavior seem difficult to me? Is there another perspective? What does my reaction say about me?

- Avoid getting emotionally involved. Ask for clarification and more information. Keep the other person talking. What do you mean by that? What more can you tell me?

- Acknowledge what the person has said. Restate what you have heard. Describe what you have heard the person say that he feels: "So what I am hearing you say is that…and it seems that you feel…"

- Ask the person to suggest how the problem could be solved: "What do you think should be done to resolve this?"

- Agree with something the other person has said, "I agree with you that…."

- Add your point of view only after you understand the other person's perspective on the problem and his or her proposed solution. (Avoid starting with *but*.) "Let me add my point of view now. I strongly feel that…"

Use the following template to work through the situation with a person whom you are experiencing as difficult.

1. What type of person are you dealing with?
2. What specific behaviors or situations give you the most trouble?
3. What is your desired state or outcome from dealing with this person?
4. What information do you have on the source(s) of this person's discontent? Or how might you acquire such information?
5. What specific techniques do you want to use to deal with the person?
6. What type of push-back do you anticipate? How can you plan for it?

Are you still feeling stuck? One manager refers to these situations as "big rocks" because they are hard to move. When you encounter "big rocks" in your journey, think back to the concept of leadership choices. Are you choosing the same old approach when you need a new one? One way to think about it is to consider constructive and destructive responses. Constructive responses move conflict to more effective resolution and destructive toward ineffective. In the conflict response chart (Figure 6.2) you can see the choices available to you.

When you choose an *active/destructive* approach you become overly emotional, lose your temper, and probably make the situation more difficult.

	Constructive	Destructive
Active	Perspective Taking Creative Solutions Expressing Emotions Reaching Out	Winning at All Costs Displaying Anger Demeaning Others Retaliating
Passive	Reflective Thinking Delay Responding Adapting	Avoiding Yielding Hiding Emotions Self Criticizing

Figure 6.2 Conflict response categories. (Reprinted with permission. Conflict Dynamics Profile ®, Eckerd College Leadership Development Institute, St. Petersburg, FL)

An *active/constructive* choice leads to setting up time in the right place to have the discussion with the other person. Preparation is a part of the active/constructive approach. Some people find that talking the situation through is a good way to get ready to resolve the issue.

Passive/constructive methods include "pausing," taking some time to get ready to talk to the other person from a position of preparedness. It could mean that you reflect and realize that you are a part of the problem and adapt your approach to the person.

Passive/destructive choices are those that avoid the problem or the person, yielding to the poor behavior, letting it happen because "There's nothing I can do about it" is a passive/destructive response that will destroy team morale, not help the individual and may result in self-criticism and lowering of your own self-esteem.

Which one of the quadrants are you using with the difficult person? Would you have more success if you moved to a different quadrant?

If you are stuck in the passive/destructive box, it may mean that you have identified a developmental obstacle in your own leadership journey. It is not easy, but you must find a way to move this "big rock" and make the rest of the journey easier.

■ Career Enhancement Tool ■
Coaching Through the Generations

Earlier in the chapter there were some generalizations about the generations. Remember that generalizations are not stereotypes. For every rule there are exceptions to the rule. When you need to coach or motivate employees from the different age groups, here are some guidelines to keep in mind.

Understanding Gen Y (born 1980–)

This group of employees grew up with the Internet. They have incredible skills to assess and apply information, giving them a sense of competence and optimism about their future. They are tech-savvy; used to quick feedback and in-

---

SCENE

A Gen Y friend, Molly, took a job with a well-respected corporation that has a reputation for being "family friendly" as well as technologically savvy. Molly does not find this to be true. She says, "I can't talk to people in higher level jobs unless my boss calls them first." She finds the company lacks friendliness and is bureaucratic. She was in the process of looking for another job. When the senior human resources team hears Molly's reaction to the company, they are shocked that anyone could find the company unfriendly. It turned out that the HR team are Baby Boomers and define "friendly" differently than Molly, the Gen Y, does. So how does Molly's boss help her? Maybe he could give Molly some project work so she has more interaction with others in the company. What are your ideas?

---

stant gratification. Multitasking is natural to them. They have had positive re-lationships with their parents and, generally, they believe they can do any-thing. They stay connected to large groups. In fact, a project with their friends is a motivator. They are service-minded, so time off to provide service is val-ued. When you coach a Gen Y, it is best to listen to hear what his or her ex-periences have been and acknowledge his or her contribution. Gen Yers are con-fident and achievement oriented. However, they want flexibility, and they want immediate feedback. They need to know their work has meaning.

Understanding Gen X (1964–1980)

Gen Xers grew up as "latch-key kids" with single-parent households. They are an independent, self-sufficient generation that is often described as cynical and pessimistic. While parents strived for self-fulfillment and monetary suc-cess, their children were left to manage on their own. Their parents, in fact, could depend on them to get things done.

═══ S C E N E ═══

Alex was told he had leadership skills, and his manager wanted him to attend the leadership academy to further prepare him for his first leadership role. Alex was critical of *every* part of the course, which met two days a week for six weeks! One of the requirements of the course was a team project. Alex's team could not decide on a proj-ect because Alex found something wrong with every idea. The team, composed of three Boomers and Alex, were ready to quit. Alex came to the instructor and said, "All of the projects they suggest are not worth doing. I don't have the time to travel to other divisions and in-terview people, which is what they want to do." And he continued, "Why would anyone want all those interviews? Will anyone pay at-tention to the data?" What's the right approach with Alex? It seems one solution would be to explain the "whys" of the project to Alex. Point out that this will help his growth too, and he could have more motivation for the project.

In order to coach this group, remember they want all the options on the table, they want answers to "why," and they want people to follow up and keep their commitments. They see time as money and, in general, don't trust management. Unlike their Boomer parents, they assume their identities when they leave work, not at work. They want respect, autonomy, skills, and a non-traditional orientation to work and life.

Understanding the Boomers (1946–1964)

The Boomers are the people who are known as the most influential generation because they are a large generation, and their sheer size has created a force in every aspect of life. They have been disillusioned with government, big business, traditional religion, and parents. Their values are self-fulfillment, individualism, and material wealth. They are unusually protective of their children and are strong idealists with passions for personal and social improvement. In the workplace, they brought us the concept of the workaholic; they brag about how many hours they work. They believe in teamwork.

In order to coach this generation, utilize their optimism. Goal attainment is one way to focus their energy. They have redefined everything and want to make the world a better place. Some are not comfortable with technology, so investigate preferences, whether phone or email. Some of them recognize that they are candidates for burnout and want relief from the long hours they have given to their organizations.

═══ S C E N E ═══

Return to the scene with Alex and look at this from the perspective of HR professionals, who happen to be Boomers. The rest of the team consisted of three people, all women, who are Boomers. Barbara, Kit, and Nancy could not believe Alex. They all had great ideas for a wonderful project that would actually result in some needed change within their organization; Alex was the only roadblock. The trio would

(continued)

(Continued)

offer workarounds to help Alex feel a part of the team, but nothing seemed to appease him. They stayed after class one day to demonstrate their desire to incorporate Alex into the team. They spoke to the instructor and asked for advice. They were trying hard not to be critical of a teammate, but they also wanted to get started. The trio feared that they would not make the deadline and would not perform well in the presentations. The instructor coached the Boomers to give Alex the space to do his part independently. With guidance from the instructor and their knowledge of Alex's work, they were able to suggest a couple of things that would build Alex's skills. Sometimes the generational preferences of teammates or direct reports can be a window into understanding why things are not working out.

Understanding the Matures (1922–1946)

This group is just about out of the traditional workplace, but many have moved into consulting or other part-time work, teaching, and working for nonprofits. They value financial security, teamwork, sacrifice, delayed gratification, and the government. They respect authority, and loyalty is one of their biggest values. They would have preferred to have a lifetime career with one employer. They work hard, are dedicated, respect rules, put duty before pleasure, and think there is a "right" way to do things.

In order to coach a mature worker, consider that he or she wants respect for the long years of work, dedication, and service. Listen to these workers to hear what their experiences have been. Acknowledge their contributions. They have a group orientation: Appeal to the best thing for the group—provide testimonials from government, business, and others in leadership roles. Emphasize that you have seen a particular approach work in the past. Allow these employees to set the "rules of the engagement," ask what has worked for them in the past, and fit your approach to that experience.

=== **S C E N E** ===

Tom retired, but has been invited back to be on a team with three other people, one from each of the other generations, who have all left the company. They are to report to management, specifying what's good about the company and what could change to make it more "friendly" to each of the generations. The four have just done introductions. The others left to go on to other jobs. Tom is the only retiree.

He considers this a great opportunity to give back to the company, as he enjoyed working there. The Gen Xer looks at his watch and says he needs to keep this moving; the Boomer steps up to lead the team; and the Gen Yer, sensing the tension, begins to wonder if it was a good idea to be on the team. Tom attempts to share his experience, but Gen X says Tom's experience is about the past, and they need to think about the future of the company. The Boomer suggests a process that should get them moving. Gen Y offers her knowledge of the company regarding flexibility; she enthusiastically puts forth an idea of a way they can collect some data to get more information for their report. The scene continues, all four of them anchored in their points of view. Tom feels critical of the others: Why can't they just work together? At this moment the organizer of the project walks in and takes a few minutes to get to know each person's backgrounds, why each left the company, and why each agreed to do the project. Within a few minutes the team is on track. Tom respects the leadership of this person; management put a good person in charge.

Personality and Leadership

Remember always that you not only have the right to be an individual, you have an obligation to be one.

—Eleanor Roosevelt

Have you ever said something like this to describe a boss or colleague: "What a micro-manager!" "He shoots from the hip" "She's so disorganized!" "Why can she just speak up more so that people hear her wonderful ideas?"

These are examples of how personalities play out at work. Your personality is the final component in your leadership mix. In the past two decades, the science of personality measurement in the workplace has developed rapidly. Research reported by the American Psychological Association and The Society for Consulting Psychology confirms that "personality is the most important factor in explaining the individual differences between leaders." [1]

═══ SCENE ═══

Albert is a successful executive; he has built a great team and is promoted to run a large division, but within a year the CEO who he reports to is disappointed. Albert's staff says that he doesn't make decisions, and he analyzes things forever. Productivity is beginning to suffer. A coach is called in to work with Albert. During the first

(continued)

(Continued)

meeting, Albert explains that he is disappointed in his staff. He wants them to work as a team, brainstorm, and collaborate on important division issues. Instead, they prefer to interact with him individually and ask for his decisions when they need them. Albert knows the value of group innovation and creativity and holds to his guns by pulling together staff meetings where he asks them to discuss current business issues. He is puzzled with their lack of participation. They are puzzled by his insistence on wasting time in group meetings. They like one-on-one interaction with him and don't see any value to sitting in a room together.

Albert is confused; his approach was extremely effective in his last job, where there was a great team spirit and excellent business results. The coach used a personality profile to help understand Albert. The profile showed that he was introverted and scored fairly low in conscientiousness, which on this profile meant that he wasn't very organized and preferred to consider many options before coming to closure.

He had a wealth of technical skills, great stress resistance, and a willingness to embrace change. However, he found it difficult to enthusiastically communicate his vision for the business or the group, partly because his underlying tendency was introversion, and he had never learned effective influencing skills and behaviors. He often failed to get complete closure on issues, thinking there was one "better" option available. While individual meetings might seem, at first glance, his preferred way to work, Albert actually preferred staff meetings; he had learned that in a group setting he could play off all the discussion and get to closure more quickly.

With some help, Albert learned that he needed to make his vision clear to his team. He worked on influencing skills and asked his assistant to help him with agendas and meeting management. He learned that the team hated coming to meetings unprepared. It turned

(continued)

(Continued)
out that Albert rarely let anyone know what he wanted them to discuss, so they were not prepared to provide input or help him make
decisions. He had to get more organized and learn how to set up
meetings so that he got the results he wanted.

This story sheds light on the issue of personality and leadership.
Personality data helped Albert to understand his strengths and weaknesses and then to learn some tools and skills to manage the things
that were not working well for him. Psychological assessment results
provide a vocabulary for describing tendencies and a view of the
"whys" behind the behaviors. This information sets the stage for more
effective employee selection, succession planning, team building, and
professional development.

The combination of scores produces a very accurate and helpful profile of
a leader's way of leading. Consider another case.

═══ **SCENE** ═══

The leader, Cory, had been told many times that others said things
like, "Not sure if he listens to us," "Not engaged in the process."
When Cory received his feedback on a personality assessment, he
had no visible reaction—he was the proverbial deer in the headlights.
When the coach asked him what he was thinking, it took Cory a
while to stammer and think his way through his reaction. Suffice it to
say he was crushed. He recited word for word what went on in every
business meeting he had attended over the last few weeks; he gave
insightful analysis to the dynamics of his team. He could not fathom
that people thought he was not listening in meetings.

What's going on? Clearly, Cory is an introvert. Extraverts want to talk everything out and in the workplace, extraverts are winning the leadership positions. In the general population, introverts and extraverts are evenly split with 49percent of the population extraverts and 51percent introverts.[2] But in the management ranks of Fortune 1000 executives, even those leaders that rate themselves as introverts at home operate as extraverts in the workplace with 71.6 percent scoring as extraverts. Often introverts are mistaken for shy or socially awkward; one of the most common misconceptions is that they are not able to give presentations or speak in public (think Johnny Carson—a famous introvert). The good news is that you can shift your behavior if you want to.

Coaching Tips for Introverts

Leaders need to be able to show that they are engaged in the process. So if you are an introvert or you manage one, here are some coaching tips that might help with this issue:

- Send agendas in advance so that introverts have time to prepare and think about topics to be discussed.
- Make sure you ask more thoughtful (internally processing) people for comments during the meeting.
- Allow for input after the meeting.
- If you tend to be quieter in meetings, make sure people know you are engaged by individually connecting with key team members before or after the session to comment on the content of the meeting.
- Thank leaders at the end of meeting and add something like: "I have some further thoughts on this. Could I send you an email when I have a chance to synthesize my ideas?"
- Learn how to interrupt more talkative people so you get your voice heard in the room.

"Derailers"—When Good Turns Bad

Leadership coaches need to help people turn weaknesses into strengths. But what happens when strengths go too far? Is it possible to have too much of a good thing?

One coach worked with a general manager, Ruben, who was a Harvard MBA. Ruben's team liked him, and management respected him for the way he managed the team and did the numbers, which was one of his strengths. But put Ruben under stress and he became obsessive, often working numbers over and over. When the company wanted to merge Ruben's division with another, the manager did not see how it could work. He did analysis after analysis to prove the idea was a bad one for his division.

Meanwhile, absent management attention, his team was in crisis. The team needed a leader to help with the people issues of a merger; they feared losing their jobs. Leadership research describes a strength-like number analysis that is overdone as a "derailer." It is the good turned bad. We all can have these traits, but some need help to manage them. Self-confidence can become arrogance; independence can turn to aloofness; conscientiousness can become worry. Here are some ways to identify and manage an asset so it doesn't become a liability.

Step 1: Identify your "derailers."

Step 2: Learn to "pause" before you act.

Step 3: Come out of your comfort zone—try a new response.

Step 4: Get balance—avoid the extremes on the scales.

In the situation above, Ruben would close his office door and run the numbers over and over again, while his employees listened to the rumors and feared the worst. Through coaching, Ruben was able to move out of his comfort zone and face the problem head on. Rather than avoid his team, he met with them and dealt with their concerns. It's important to realize how your strengths can derail you.

You do not necessarily need coaching or an assessment to identify your derailers. You may know yourself well enough to know if you use any of these techniques when you are under stress. It might help to look at a list of derailers with their corresponding strengths.

Derailer	Corresponding Strength
False advocate (passive resistance)	Calm and dependable
Worrier	Analytical, prudent, wise
Cynic	Risk aware
Rule breaker	Innovative, flexible, creative
Perfectionist	Excellence
Egotist	Self-confidence
Pleaser	Great people skills
Hyper-moody	Exciting
Detached	Calm, reserved, quiet
Upstager	Impressive impact
Eccentric	Innovative and creative

Source: CDR Assessment Group. (1998). *CDR Leadership Risk Assessment Report®*. Tulsa, OK: Author. Used with permission.

Does it help you to find the derailers most in your comfort zone? These patterns will show up time and again when you are in a crisis situation. For example, Ruben, the analytical general manager, was likely rewarded at the Harvard Business School for his analysis. However, as a general manager, the behavior was no longer an asset, and he was out of balance since he did not connect with his division and provide leadership during a crisis.

If you are promoted, you should be aware that things that worked in the past might not fit in the new world. The tricky part is that you likely have had positive or no feedback on these behaviors early in your career, then suddenly they will surface as derailers. Leaders often fall back on the traits that brought them success earlier in their careers rather than develop the skills that will work at the higher level of leadership. Sometimes a trait that was seen as innovative or creative early on comes across as aloofness or eccentricity as the leader gains success. Can you see why a big ego works in a sales role to help manage the constant rejection, but as a Vice President of Sales that same ego seems like arrogance and ignoring the troops? According to research done at the Center for Creative Leadership, 30 to 50 percent of high potential leaders get off track in their leadership—that's an incredible statistic.[3] Failure among CEOs is even higher. A personality report can help you so you don't get on the derailment track.

══ SCENE ══

You need Abigail Sample to do HR work. She is assigned to a group and is to provide hiring, benefits, compensation, succession, and training support. The personality report shows that Abigail is intense, self-critical, and doesn't work well under pressure; she is not at all interested in taking on a leadership role. However, she is outgoing and enjoys social interaction. Abigail is task-focused and not empathetic to others; she is potentially creative, adaptable, and inventive. She is clever and imaginative, as well as a fairly hands-on learner. How might these strengths become weaknesses under stress? Abigail is motivated by a good time. She has a good sense of humor, she definitely is creative, and you have noted that she loves technology. She has told colleagues that she likes HR because she makes a positive difference in people's lives. Can you picture Abigail developing a technology approach to meeting some of the needs of her customers? Do you see her taking on the social events for HR? Can you imagine that she could manage the administrative side of her job more effectively if the systems were there to support her?

Abigail has been part of a selection process for a new leader of the technology area. The leader is coming from a job in a local university where he has been very successful; however, he has not worked in a corporate job before.

(continued)

(Continued)

One way to avoid the pain of derailment is to plan the transition into a new job with more care. Human Resources may provide a service called "Team Assimilation." Here is an example of a how Abigail, the HR manager, could help the new hire, Rami, assimilate. Abigail welcomes Rami to the organization and does quite a bit to get him on board and working effectively with his team. She uses a leader assimilation. Nine months later, she thinks it might be a good time to reevaluate the situation. In the team assimilation meeting, the team communicates that they think Rami needs to do less individual decision making, be more visible to his direct reports, and that the team needs to "connect" with Rami more on an informal basis, so they have more opportunities to talk.

Abigail sees an opportunity to strive for excellence by taking the process to the next level. She asks Rami if he would be interested in taking a personality profile. She feels that the personality information would be enlightening to Rami. She is correct. The profile shows he rated a 10 out of a possible 100 on a Sociability Scale. Rami clearly did not enjoy social interactions. Conversely, he rated a perfect 100 on the scale that measures "Detachment," which means Rami has a big tendency to withdraw, preferring to think things through on his own. The combined set of data allows Rami and his team to truly understand their issues and work toward change.

Assimilation Process

If you want to plan a new leader and team assimilation, here are the steps for doing it.

Step 1: HR contacts the new leader to recommend and explain the assimilation process.

(If HR doesn't contact you, go see them; see if you can introduce the idea to the organization.)

Step 2: The new leader invites the staff by letter (email) to attend an assimilation meeting and clarifies the objectives/reasons for having it.

Step 3: The new leader usually kicks off the assimilation, explaining the objectives and reasons for having the meeting.

Step 4: HR facilitates the meeting, which provides feedback on how the leader is perceived.

Step 5: It is possible to partner with a consultant and develop a personality profile.

If you haven't been able to identify your own risk factors, then pay attention to the impact you are having on others and notice when you get "ineffective" responses. You might be able to identify what needs to change. You are likely experiencing the risk factor as a positive because you were rewarded for that behavior earlier in your life. One executive actually looked at the feedback and commented about the negative feedback this way, "Oh, he must have been having a bad day that day. This can't be what he really thinks." A few months later, she left the company.

▓ Career Enhancement Tool ▓
Resiliency

Setbacks come in all sizes: They can slow you down and cause you to lose focus, self-confidence, and the ability to produce the best results.

When you experience a setback, you need to recover, to get back to normal; the longer you stay in a less-than-optimum state, the more it affects your ability to perform. Athletes train for dealing with setbacks. Resiliency can make the difference between success and failure, between moving forward and standing still.

Unfortunately, in the corporate world, a series of setbacks takes an employee out of contention for the next level. In reality, successful careers are shaped by both personal and professional failures. Leaders who can help their employees respond with resilience ensure their unit's successfulness. Much like an athlete's coach, at the worst times, leaders provide a difference.

> ===== **S C E N E** =====
>
> One of your teammates, Bridget, comes to talk; she is devastated. A few months ago, she had her second child, and she cut back to three days of work per week with two of those days from home. At a company social event last night, she learned that her boss and other people on the team interviewed a really great person to work in her department. Bridget knows that if this person is hired, she will be demoted. What really upsets Bridget is that no one told her about these interviews or the open position. Now that she works from home, she gets left out of a lot of important information. No one seems to want to include her in the information that is critical to the department. She works harder than she ever did when she came into the office every day, but it seems to go unnoticed; instead, the boss pressures her to tell him when she can increase the number of days in the office. Bridget feels that her future with the company has ended. The company allowed for the flexibility of working at home but now they are not supporting her or the policy. As Bridget's teammate you want to help.

Reframing

The first thing to do is help Bridget reframe the experience. Look at the facts with Bridget. This is a skill where leaders move employees from pessimism to optimism. Pessimists always latch on to the worst of all causes for any event. By moving toward a more optimistic outlook, a leader helps his or her employees see that maybe there is a way to reframe this event in a more positive light. You ask Bridget, "How do you know that you will be demoted?" "Have you talked with the boss about this?" In other words, you help the person check out the facts: How did she arrive at the beliefs and consequences she has?

People often resort to a distorted interpretation of the situation; your goal is to offer a new lens to view the situation. When someone comes to you upset about something, notice what she has made prominent. So often managers say things like, "Bridget, that's just plain silly, you are not going to get demoted." Try to avoid discounting the person or attempting to talk her out of her position. Instead, reframe the discussion from the negative to the positive. "It sounds like you are upset that we have not talked with you about the departmental changes we might make." This will allow your employees a chance to become more resilient.

Conclusion

What will you need to lead in the future? The business world changes so quickly, no one can be sure of what the next decade will bring. But the i4cp report called *Leading into the Future*[1] summarized where it sees the future:

> We think there will be more shared leadership and that lateral and peer-based relationships will be critical to success. We know that women are better at using networks. So will women finally have the opportunity to really show their stuff over the next ten years? Information systems are also bound to have a continuing impact on leadership. We think that leaders will become more disciplined about the importance of leading.

Virtual and remote work will require that leaders show discipline in building trust, motivating, managing performance, and getting work accomplished. Leading at a distance leaves very little room for building trust. The job of leader requires the ability to blend classic management techniques with cross-cultural knowledge and to withstand increased scrutiny while delivering bottom-line results. What you will need in the future is an ability to adapt and be resilient. Learn to be open to change. Leaders with strong business acumen understand how to assess the business environment and use that knowledge to their firm's competitive advantage and to help create their own lasting leadership legacy.

The best leaders model their values each and every day, not just in words, but in their actions. Creating a legacy is not simply what the leader does, but how others interpret those actions. So in order to leave a lasting legacy, a leader must demonstrate motives and values. Reflect on your impact, assess your behavior, and determine how your personality affects the people around you. In order to continue your leadership journey, share these models and assessments with your manager and those who report to you. Work each day to make your choices active and constructive. Take a few minutes to reflect where the decisions you made today fall on that continuum and what you might do differently tomorrow. Simply put, think about ways to increase behaviors on the effective side and decrease behaviors on the ineffective side.

Leaders make choices all day long, and, of course, they won't always be good choices, but through practice you will see that you increase the frequency of good choices you make. Ultimately, building your team and your leadership legacy is integral to get the results you desire. While those who perform well are seen as self-sacrificing, when you put what's best for the organization or the group ahead of your own needs, you can build consensus and make a difference among the people on your team and in your organization. So, begin right now to reflect on your choices that grow the business, other people, and yourself. Good luck to you on the journey!

Notes

Introduction

1. Bear, Donna, Dennis, Donna, Forcade, James W., et al. (2005, October 6). *Leading into the future: A global study of leadership: 2005–2015*, American Management Association/Institute for Corporate Productivity. For more information visit www.amanet.org

Chapter 1

1. Horner, M. (1997). Leadership theory: Past, present and future. *Team Performance Management, 3* (4), 270–287. MCB University Press, Heriot-Wyatt University, Edinburgh, Scotland.

2. Gardner, Howard. (1983). *Frames of mind: A theory of multiple intelligences.* New York: Basic Books.

3. Goleman, Daniel. (1994). *Emotional intelligence.* New York: Bantam Books.

4. Brinkmeyer, Kim, & Rybicki, S.L. (1998, August). *The dark-side of normal personality: New perspectives for workplace decisions.* Paper presented at the 106th annual convention of the American Psychological Association, San Francisco, CA.

5. Burns, J.M. (1978). *Leadership.* New York: Harper & Row.

6. Bass, B.M., & Avolio, B.J., (1990).The implications of transactional and transformational leadership for individual, team, and organizational development. In R.W. Woodman & W. A. Passmore (Eds.), *Research in organizational change and development* (pp. 231–272). Greenwich, CT: JAI.

7. Pearce, C.L., & Conger, J.A. (Eds.). (2003). *Shared leadership: Reframing the how's and why's of leadership.* Thousand Oaks, CA: Sage Publications.

8. Avolio, B., & Yammarino, F.J. (Eds.). (2002). *Transformational and charismatic leadership: The road ahead.* Oxford, UK: Elsevier Science.

9. Kouzes, J.M., & Posner, B.Z. (2003).*Credibility: How leaders gain and lose it, why people demand it.* San Francisco: Jossey Bass Publishing.

10. Dirks, K.T., & Ferrin, D.L. (2001). The role of trust in organizational settings. *Organization Science*, 12, 450–467.

Chapter 2

1. Wheelan, S.A. (2005). *Creating effective teams: A guide for members and leaders.* Thousand Oaks, CA: Sage Publications.
2. Avolio, B. (1999). *Full leadership development: Building the vital forces in organizations.* Thousand Oaks, CA: Sage Publications.
3. Wheelan, op. cit.
4. Retrieved from www.riskmetrics.com September, 2008.
5. Ibid.
6. Ibid.

Chapter 3

1. Iowa State University: College of Family and Consumer Sciences. Retrieved in September 2008, from www.fcs.iastate.edu/classweb/Fall2003/TC165/notes/stereotype.pdf
2. Leary, M. (1996). *Self-presentation: Impression management and interpersonal behavior.* Boulder, CO: Westview Press.
3. Sojeski, K.S., Reilly, R., & Dominick, P. (2006). *The role of virtual distance in innovation and success.* Proceedings of the 39th Hawaii International Conference on Systems Sciences, IEEE (Institute of Electrical and Electronics Engineers, Inc.).
4. Jarvenpaa, S.L., & Leidner, D.E. (1999, June). Communication and trust in global virtual teams. *Organization and Science, 10* (6), 791–815.

Chapter 4

1. Lattimore, R. (Trans.). (1961). *The Iliad of Homer.* Chicago: University of Chicago Press.

Chapter 5

1. Horstein, H., & de Guerre, H. (2006, March/April). Bureaucratic organizations are bad for your health. *Ivey Business Journal,* Ottawa, Canada.

2. Kulsea, P. (2007, February). Engaging leaders on a gender level. *Chief Learning Officer*, 52–55.

3. Gallup Organization. *Creating a highly engaged and productive workplace culture.* Available through www.gallup.com

4. Vickers, M., Dennis, D.J., Tompson, H., Lindberg, A., & Williams, R. (2008, November). *Cultivating effective cultures.* St. Petersburg, FL: Institute for Corporate Productivity.

Chapter 6

1. McConnell, C.R. (2005). Motivating your employees and yourself. *The Health Care Manager, 24* (3), 284–292.

2. Gottman, J.M. (1998, February). Psychology and the study of marital processes. *Annual Review of Psychology, 49,* 169–197.

3. Fredrickson, B.L., & Losada, M.F. (2005, October). Positive affect and the complex dynamics of human flourishing. *American Psychologist, 60* (7), 678–686.

4. Rath, T., & Clifton, D.O. (2004). *How full is your bucket?* New York: Gallup Press.

Chapter 7

1. McCormick, I., & Burch, J.B. (2008, September). Personality-focused coaching for leadership development. *Consulting Psychology Journal: Practice and Research, 60* (3), 267–276.

2. Myers, P.D., & Myers, K.B. (2001). *Snapshots of the 16 types,* Palo Alto, CA: Consulting Psychologists Press.

3. Lombardo, M.M., & Eichinger, R.W. (1995). *Preventing derailment: What to do before it's too late.* Greensboro, NC: Center for Creative Learning.

Conclusion

1. Bear, D., Dennis, D.J., Forcade, J.W., et al. (2005). *Leading into the future: A global study of leadership: 2005–2015.* St. Petersburg, FL: Institute for Corporate Productivity.

Bibliography

Bass, B., Avolio, B., Jung, D., & Berson, Y. (2003). Predicting unit performance by assessing transformational and transactional leadership. *Journal of
Applied Psychology, 88* (2), 297–218.

Benson, R., Furst, S., & Blackburn, R. (2006, Summer). Training for virtual
teams: An investigation of current practices and future needs. *Human Resource Management, 45* (2), 229–247. On line Wiley InterScience www.
interscience.wiley.com

Chemers, M.M. (2000). Leadership research and theory: A functional integra-
tion. *Group Dynamics Theory, Research, and Practice, 4* (1), 27–43.

Davis, W., & Gardner, W.L. (2004). Perceptions of politics and organizational
cynicism: An attributional and leader-member exchange perspective. *Science Direct,* Elsevier, Inc.

Feeling valued is the best motivation. (2008). *Human Resource Management
International Digest, 16* (3).

Hawley, C. (2001). *100+ tactics for office politics.* Hauppauge, NY: Barrons
Educational Series.

Horner, M. (2007). Leadership theory: Past, present and future. *Team Performance Management, 3* (4), 270–287.

Institute for Corporate Productivity. (2005). *Leading into the future. Survey and
Report.* St. Petersburg, FL: Author.

Lindberg, A. (2007). *Corporate culture: A highlight report.* St. Petersburg, FL:
Institute for Corporate Productivity.

Reina, D., & Reina, M.L. (2007). *Trust and betrayal in the workplace: Building effective relationships in your organization* (2nd ed.). San Francisco, CA:
Berrett-Koehler Publishers.

Ulrich, D., & Smallwood, N. (2007). *Five steps to building your personal leadership brand.* Boston: Harvard Business School Publishing Corporation.

Wiley, C. (1997). What motivates employees according to over 40 years of motivation surveys. *International Journal of Manpower, 18* (3), 263–280.

Zaleznik, A. (2004, January). Managers and leaders: Are they different? *Harvard Business Review, 82* (1), 74–81.

RECOMMENDED READING/RESOURCES

This resource list has been divided up into six sections: transformational leadership, group development, influencing and negotiating, politics, motivation and dealing with difficult people, leadership personality and derailment.

Transformational Leadership

Avolio, B., (1999). *Full leadership development.* Thousand Oaks, CA: Sage Publications.

Avolio, B., & Luthans, F. (2006). *The high impact leader.* New York: McGraw-Hill.

Avolio, B., & Yammarino, F. (Eds.). (2002). *Transformational and charismatic leadership: The road ahead.* Oxford, UK: Elsevier Science, Ltd.

Bass, B. (1998). *Transformational leadership.* Mahwah, NJ: Lawrence Erlbaum.

Bass, B., & Riggio, R.E. (2006). *Transformational leadership* (2nd ed.). Mahwah, NJ: Lawrence Erlbaum.

Pearce, C.L., & Conger, J.A. (Eds). (2003). *Shared leadership: Reframing the hows and whys of leadership.* Thousand Oaks, CA: Sage Publications.

Group Development

Belbin, M.R. (1999). *Management teams: Why they succeed or fail.* Oxford, UK: Butterworth-Heinemann.

Bens, I. (2000). *Facilitating with ease.* San Francisco, CA: Jossey-Bass Publishers.

Buzan, T. (2003). *Head first.* New York: Thorsons, HarperCollins.

Wageman, R., Nunes, D., Burruss, J., & Hackman, J.R. (2008). *Senior leadership teams: What it takes to make them great.* Boston: Harvard Business School Publishing Corporation.

Wheelan, S. (2005). *Creating effective teams* (2nd ed.). Thousand Oaks, CA: Sage Publications.

Woods, K., & Uden, I. (2007). *Meeting magic.* Oxfordshire, UK: Meeting Magic Publications. (www.meetingmagic.co.uk)

Influencing and Negotiating

Bellman, G. (2001). *Getting things done when you are not in charge.* San Francisco: Berrett-Koehler Publishers.

Shister, N. (1997). *10 minute guide to negotiating.* New York: Macmillan Spectrum/Alpha Books.

Politics

Ferris, G.R., Davidson, S.L., & Perrewe, P.L. (2005). *Political skill at work.* Mountain View, CA: Davies Black Publishing.

Hawley, C. *(2001). 100+ tactics for office politics.* Hauppauge, NY: Barrons Educational Series.

Motivation and Dealing with Difficult People

Bacon, T.R. (2006). *What people want.* Mountain View, CA: Davies Black Publishing.

Brinkman, R., & Kirschner, R. (1994). *Dealing with people you can't stand.* New York: McGraw-Hill.

Daniels, A.C. (2000). *Bringing out the best in people.* New York: McGraw-Hill.

Green, T., & Hayes, M. (1993). *Belief system: The secret to motivation and improved performance.* Winston Salem, NC: Beechwood Press.

Lancaster, L.C., & Stillman, D. (2002). *When generations collide.* New York: HarperCollins.

Raines, C. (2003). *Connecting generations.* Berkeley, CA: Crisp Publications.

Silberman, M., & Hansburg, F. (2000). *People smart: Developing your interpersonal intelligence.* San Francisco, CA: Berrett-Koehler Publishers.

Tracy, D., & Morin, W.J. (2001). *Truth, trust, and the bottom line.* Chicago: Dearborn Financial Publishing.

Tulgan, B. (2007). *It's okay to be the boss.* New York: HarperCollins.

Wall, B. (2008). *Working relationships: Using emotional intelligence to enhance your effectiveness with others.* Mountain View, CA: Davies Black Publishing.

Leadership Personality and Derailment

Dotlitch, D., & Cairo, P. (2003). *Why CEO's fail: The 11 behaviors that can derail your climb to the top and how to manage them.* San Francisco, CA: Jossey-Bass Publishers.

Reivich, K., & Shatte, A. (2003). *The resilience factor.* New York: Random House.

Index

About the Author

Donna J. Dennis, PhD.

Donna is a coach, a consultant, and a researcher. For the past six years, she has been Managing Partner of *Leadership Solutions Consulting*, LLC, a consulting firm focused on customized responses to individual, team, and organization challenges. She pioneered the firm's innovative "solutions-based coaching," which is designed to meet the needs of managers who want to gain skills and competencies quickly, efficiently, and cost effectively.

Earlier in her career, Donna worked for nine years teaching in academia (The Wharton Business School, the University of Pennsylvania, and Rider University, Parkland College). She also worked in organizations for twenty years as a Leadership and Organization Development professional with RCA, GE, The Hospital of the University of Pennsylvania, Chubb Insurance, and C.R. Bard, Inc. Donna currently spends part of her time supporting the research projects of *i4cp* (The Institute for Corporate Productivity) and teaching. She teaches "Building Effective Professional Relationships" at the Gestalt International Study Center and a variety of leadership courses for the American Management Association.

Donna received her B.S. and M.S. in Education from the University of Illinois and her Ph.D. in Human and Organization Development from The Fielding Graduate Institute. She has earned numerous certifications and completed advanced training in Coaching through the Gestalt International Study Center.

Apply what you learned in this book—in an interactive environment with your peers!

Get $200 off the price of this seminar. (Mention code LCC7)

Preparing for Leadership:
What It Takes to Take the Lead

SEMINAR #2536

Hands-on leadership training can help take you to the next level in your career. Learn how to get noticed and selected for a leadership position and develop the skills every confident leader needs.

This AMA leadership training course is uniquely designed to help leaders-to-be get ready for their new challenges and responsibilities. You'll discover the heart, soul and mind of true leadership. Through role-playing, self-assessment tests and other leadership training scenarios, you'll explore leadership roles as strategist, change agent, coach, manager, communicator, mentor and team member. And you'll learn how to develop your unique leadership style for maximum impact.

WHO SHOULD ATTEND
Any manager who needs leadership training to step into a leadership role or who is about to take on a new leadership assignment.

HOW YOU WILL BENEFIT
- Project a more dynamic image
- Discover your own unique leadership style
- Determine which leadership attributes you already possess
- Apply lessons learned through leadership training to take on your first leadership position with greater confidence
- Get noticed by learning how to look and talk like a leader
- Apply lessons learned through leadership training to refine your skills in gaining and using power and influence positively
- Learn how to motivate a team, including "difficult people"
- Protect yourself against the pitfalls of intra-organizational politics

This Seminar Features Blended Learning
AMA Blended Learning combines instructor-led training with online pre- and post-seminar assessments, tune-up courses and other resources to maximize your training goals. Through a blend of proven instructor-led seminars and powerful online technology, AMA Blended Learning provides a compelling and more comprehensive experience for the learner—producing a greater return-on-investment for the employer and the seminar participant.

For complete seminar content and schedule information, call **1-800-262-9699** or visit **www.amanet.org**

American Management Association
www.amanet.org